SEND ME

STORIES OF ORDINARY PEOPLE
PLANTING NEW CHURCHES

EDITED BY
JOHN MCGINLEY

The Gregory Centre for Church Multiplication
ccx.org.uk

Send Me

First published in 2022 by The Gregory Centre for Church Multiplication

www.ccx.org.uk

Editor John McGinley

Cover Design by Grandslam Studio Ltd

Typeset by Revo Creative Ltd

ISBN 978-1-8384743-4-8

eISBN 978-1-8384743-3-1

Printed in the United Kingdom

First Edition 2022

1 2 3 4 5 6 7 8 9 10

I find these stories of how new church communities are earthed and birthed by lay planters to be deeply inspiring. I don't understand why we put up so many barriers to gathering as Christians in local communities to worship God and love our neighbourhoods. If God is calling you, then go and plant – God will equip you, and I trust that the Church of England will catch up and support you eventually!

RT REVD DR JOANNE GRENFELL, Bishop of Stepney

Send Me *is an inspiring collection of 16 stories of courageous women and men that have discerned a local need and stepped out in response to God's call. You cannot help but smile as you read the stories of the transforming power of God at work in these communities. I encourage you to read this book and as you do, listen out for God's prompting. He might just be calling you too.*

RT REVD DR RIC THORPE, Bishop of Islington

How exciting to read these stories of people building Christian community in estates, rural villages, and inner city, among ex-offenders, people with learning disabilities, and many who just never thought that church could be for them. If you are ever tempted to think church planting in the UK is about replicating trendy worship, read this book. Motivated by the transformation Christ has brought to their own lives, 16 planters explain how they have answered God's call to share his love. Thank you to them, to the volunteers who work with them, and to the courageous clergy whose support made their journey possible.

VEN CANON SALLY GAZE, Archdeacon for Rural Mission, Diocese of St Edmundsbury and Ipswich

God's primary instrument for the transformation of society is the local church. These stories show that. But they tell of how God calls people like us to be agents of his grace. Here are stories of faith and obedience, vulnerability and risk, joy and hope. And I trust it leaves many wondering that if God can do this through these people, what might he desire to do through us . . .

REVD CANON CHRIS RUSSELL, Archbishop of Canterbury's Adviser for Evangelism and Witness

The Church has entered an exciting new era and John has gathered timely powerful stories of how we are creatively shifting in these days. These journeys will inspire you to hear and step fully into the call of God on your life, moving with the wind of his Spirit to perhaps dream and begin to see the creative expression of Church he has called you to release in this hour.

REVD ANNE CALVER, Unleashed Overseer

In a world that knows so much darkness, here are 16 stories bursting with the Light of Christ as ordinary women and men step out in faith to do extraordinary things with God and for God. The oft-repeated refrain in the stories of the power of prayer to open doors and change circumstances is a challenge to us all to pray more boldly as we seek to humbly share the good news of Jesus with the world.

REVD NICK MCKEE, Blackburn Director of Vocations and Chair of the M:Power Project Board

This book contains some great stories! They will warm your heart and inspire you. As one contributor said, anyone can do the sort of thing described here. Just find a friend, pray together about how you can love the people round you, build relationships with them, share your experiences of Jesus (the book contains some easy-to-copy examples), and see what the Holy Spirit does!

REVD DR MICHAEL MOYNAGH, author, advocate, and consultant on new Christian communities

These are brilliantly encouraging stories from faith-filled and faithful people who were willing to step out, develop relationships with others, and see what God does. They show what a beautiful tapestry the Holy Spirit can create as the people of God develop a mixed ecology of church bringing glory to our Lord Jesus.

REVD GARETH ROBINSON, Rector, St Philips Chapel Street and Head of Church Planting Training for New Wine England

If you ever wondered if you could pioneer a new church community, then read this book. The stories of ordinary people doing extraordinary things will inspire you to get started.

REVD PHIL HOYLE, Pioneer Enabler for London, CCX

CONTENTS

ACKNOWLEDGEMENTS

The heroines and heroes of this book are the people who stepped forward, risked failure, overcame obstacles, loved and served sacrificially, and enabled a new church community to form. In giving time to tell their story, they have shown again their generosity and I am extremely grateful. Their stories would have remained hidden in their locations if it were not for Ros Hoare's ability to connect with them and ask questions and notice what God is doing. Gill Troup then captured them through conducting interviews and writing the stories in a way that the voices of the church planters are heard so authentically and engagingly. And the publication of a book never happens without the work of designing, editing, and setting the text and I am grateful to Jo Stockdale and Chelsea Hayes for this work.

Send Me is part of the work of Myriad, which is seeking to serve the mixed ecology vision of the Church of England in which new forms of church community will be planted alongside parish churches to reach their communities with the gospel of Jesus Christ. Bishop Ric Thorpe oversees this work, as part of the Gregory Centre for Church Multiplication, and I am grateful for his vision and leadership that has established and enabled this significant contribution to all that God is doing within his Church at this time.

FOREWORD

One of the greatest privileges of my ministry as a bishop has been the moments of discernment of how God's grace is growing in a person's life, and then enabling and supporting them to step further into what God is calling them to. The stories in this book are wonderful examples of this. They remind me of when Revd Ben Woodfield came to me with a desire to build on his experience as a pioneer curate and establish a network which would support the training and growth of new church communities; small congregations where the local leadership would be lay, with priestly oversight at the network level. From that process of discernment of the call of God, the Antioch Network was born. With some financial investment from the Strategic Development Unit and a diocesan-wide Bishops' Mission Order giving permission for new communities to form anywhere in the diocese (though always working with the support of the local parish), Ben and John Brett have already overseen the formation of 11 new churches in some of the poorest communities in our diocese. What flows from these new churches are stories of lives transformed and beautiful acts of love and service. Increasingly, I am seeing people brought to faith in the Antioch Network adding their contributions to the wider life of our diocese.

People sometimes wonder why this kind of venture and new pattern of ministry is necessary. The principle of the incarnation takes us to the heart of it as we follow the example of Christ who, as the apostle John describes, 'made his dwelling among us' (John 1:14). Worshipping communities often start when people sense a call to express the love of Christ with the people around them in the places where they live and work. The church can empower them to 'incarnate' Christ's love in a way that will connect with people there. That's why we need a mixed ecology church with parish churches alongside new worshipping communities. Within *Send Me* is the story from Manchester Diocese of Trinity Community Church which was commissioned from Holy Trinity, Platt. It has since multiplied into two congregations, serving the communities of Fallowfield and Rusholme so that now these communities have a local church living and serving them.

The formation of new church communities to carry the love of Christ to their local communities is clearly a work of the Spirit. I am delighted that *Send Me* captures some of these stories and pray that as you read it you will be inspired to step forward into all God is calling.

RT REVD DR DAVID WALKER

Bishop of Manchester

INTRODUCTION

Welcome to *Send Me*, a collection of 16 wonderful stories of what happens when people hear the call of Jesus Christ to plant a new church community. When we hear about God doing amazing things through someone who we can relate to, something powerful happens within us. Suddenly the impossible becomes possible, imagination is released, and what God might be calling us to opens up. These stories are written to inform and inspire you with what God is doing in his Church in England in our time. And they are inviting you to join in.

And there is a bigger picture that all of this fits into. The Church of England has established a strategy and vision to be a 'mixed ecology' church, where a rich variety of many new worshipping communities will complement the existing parish churches. As this picture of the future developed, The Gregory Centre for Church Multiplication formed Myriad, a team of people focussed on serving this vision. Myriad aims to shine a light on the new forms of church and leadership that are emerging and to provide training and support for people looking to plant new church communities.

As part of this work, the Myriad team conducted some research by engaging with people who had led the formation of a new church community as a lay person. The 'Listening to the Voice of the Lay Planters Report' shows that lay people are already planting churches within and across the Church of England and it captured their stories and the lessons that can be learned from their experience. And we were so inspired by all that we were discovering that we wanted others to be able to hear these stories for themselves.

The lay people who God called to do this work come from rural and urban areas across England and are women and men of different ages and different social and ethnic backgrounds. That in itself is powerful as these stories shatter any preconceptions of the 'ideal' church leader, expanding our understanding of how God works and whom he anoints and calls to lead within his church.

There are threads of similar experiences and practices that run through many of the stories. These include the prayerfulness of this work, as small groups of people prayer-walk their area longing for God to transform their neighbourhood and seeking to discern what he is calling them to do. They describe the joy of forming community, eating together, and seeing the surprising people God is at work in. Many of the lay people faced great challenges in this work and this made the wider support from clergy and the parish churches even more important. These new forms of church are emerging from the established Church and there are some beautiful testimonies of people finding faith in Jesus Christ as a result of the church being formed in new ways and places that connected with them.

In Scripture, the metaphor of 'first-fruits' helps us to understand that the work of God often starts in a small way, but these small beginnings are the first signs of the harvest that is coming. I believe these stories are the first-fruits of what we will see God do in his Church in the UK in coming years and that they help us to understand something of what this might look like. In Revelation 19:10, the apostle John records these words: 'It is the Spirit of prophecy who bears testimony to Jesus.' So as someone testifies of what God has done in their life, they not only give him glory but their words also speak prophetically that God can and wants to do this again. As I read these stories, I have that sense of God wanting to do something like this again and again and again in every city, town, and village across our nation.

In the Gregory Centre, we are gripped by the ongoing call of Jesus to go and make disciples and the urgent need for the re-evangelisation of our nation. Forming new church communities, which will live out the gospel and incarnate it in different contexts, will be key in this work. My prayer is that, as you read these stories, you will sense the Spirit saying: 'Whom shall I send?' and you will be able to respond by saying: 'Here I am Lord, send me.'

REVD CANON JOHN MCGINLEY

Executive Director, Myriad

FIONA MAYNE

Haywood Village Church, Weston-super-Mare

Ten years ago, Revd Fiona Mayne was an atheist and there was no church in Haywood Village, where she now lives. It was a village in name only, a new housing estate under construction. Now an ordained deacon, soon to be priest, Fiona is leading a church at the heart of this new community and shares her journey which includes an astounding offer from the estate's developer.

Growing up, I always thought that the Bible was a collection of fairy tales and nice stories. I didn't realise it had any basis at all in truth. As a child, I found church to be quite dusty and dark; I didn't find any joy there. Aged 40, I was far from God, living a materialistic and selfish life as an independent financial adviser. I didn't believe in God, nor did I even think about him.

As a single parent, my sister recommended a Christian hotel as a safe, friendly place to go on holiday. Despite being an atheist, I booked, with some trepidation, to go to Sidholme, a Christian Guild hotel in Sidmouth. The people there were kind and welcoming and didn't try to force God on me so I needn't have worried!

I went on a few of these trips and it was during one holiday that I had a 'Damascus moment.' We were sitting around the table at dinner one night, discussing faith, and something in my heart just changed. I suddenly knew for the first time that God was real. The next day I looked in the mirror and saw a different me. I liked myself for the first time and felt a joy and inner peace that I had never known before. I felt compelled to buy a Bible.

Going home, I felt I couldn't wait to tell everyone what had happened, not to force faith on people but just to give them the chance to encounter God, because I was so glad that someone had told me about him. I think my biggest step was in 2012: I wanted to know more about Jesus and so I took myself to a local Alpha course.[1] It was while I was there that a desire to serve God in my local community started to grow.

About six months later, I met Revd Tom Yacomeni, who was curate at St Paul's in Weston-super-Mare. He was considering taking a role as lead minister at Locking Castle Church, two miles from Haywood Village. Tom's role involved pioneer outreach work to new communities and he wanted to get an Alpha course going as soon as possible. I told him, 'I know everyone! I've lived here nearly 10 years.' So, we had this big community barbeque at my house, about 100 people came, and I just introduced everyone to Tom and the team. That was really the first time I stepped out and told all my neighbours I was a Christian.

Over the next two years I led Alpha and helped run community events organised by the church and a newly formed residents' association at Haywood Village. Locking Castle became my 'sending church' as I learned more and more about mission and evangelism and different approaches to outreach and pioneer ministry.

I kept feeling this calling to Haywood Village and I didn't really know why. I'd find myself driving there – I lived five minutes away – and feeling a real heart for the place. It was just something I couldn't ignore. Over time, I got to know people, just walking my dog, and I became a school governor and joined the Women's Institute.

I kept feeling this calling to Haywood Village and I didn't really know why.

I began to ask people who lived there what they wanted for the estate and the answer was always the same: somewhere to meet up. I felt God was calling me to gather community – God-centred community – because there

1 www.alpha.org.uk

was nothing here at all, just fields and one pub right at the other end of the estate, and empty of people during the day as most commuted to work. I love building community, creating places where people can come together and flourish. Hospitality is something I love too.

So I started the Take Five pop-up café with a group of people, some from Locking Castle Church and some from other local churches. It ran one afternoon a week in the school's community room. The café grew and grew and we were having about 100 people come along. There were crafts and dressing-up and table tennis and Lego – it was absolute chaos!

I think you need to be upfront about faith, putting your flag in the ground and saying, 'This is what we're about.' So with the café, everyone knows we're Christians, I haven't ever been apologetic about faith, and we invite people to everything the church is running. But I haven't ever forced it on people either. We encourage everyone to come to the café whether they are interested in church or not, and there's never any Christian content there because that might put people off.

We encourage everyone to come to the café whether they are interested in church or not.

As a result of café conversations and friendships, I started an Alpha group and then a group which just naturally formed from the people who'd been on Alpha, like a homegroup. Some of those people who were interested in faith said: 'You're all Christians; where's the church in Haywood Village?' I said there wasn't one yet but if there was one, what would they like it to be? It was very much getting people to tell me what they wanted to do but still keeping it authentic, which is important. People said they'd like it to be like the café but with a Christian content, which I thought was fair enough!

So we started Tea and Toast Church in the sports hall in café format, once a month. It was a lot about hospitality – the smell of toast is so homely, isn't it? – and about sharing our lives together, discussing the Bible, and asking questions. Soon there were people who wanted to go deeper and meet every week. So again, I asked the group what that would look like, keeping it authentic and not just a social club. It's not changing the message, it's just the way people hear it. We came up with a weekly group on a Wednesday night, called Rooted. We eat together and read the Bible and discuss the passage in the context of our own lives and what that means to us. Then we pray and sometimes sing worship songs. That's gone really well.

When I started the Take Five café, Tom Yacomeni was such an encouragement to me. He had a remit for church planting as part of his role at St Paul's and he was very much a supporter and facilitator, so he would let me get on with it. We managed to get a grant for five hours' work a week, which got me started and able to move away from my financial adviser work a bit more. Tom guided me all the way through and helped me to imagine I could lead a church on the estate. 'You can take everything you've done so far and go and start a church there,' he said. And I was like, wow! I didn't even think of that. Church planting was completely new to me.

Tom guided me all the way through and helped me to imagine I could lead a church on the estate.

In some ways, we're not like some other church plants because of the way we've emerged and evolved. We start with where people are, rather than taking a model of church and planting something exactly the same on a new site. We're not too formal and we try to avoid Christian jargon. Rather than spotlighting people and asking them, 'Do you have a faith?' – because that can make people feel awkward and intimidated – we just share our lives and faith. Everyone is welcome to join anything, wherever they are on their journey. I feel I'm a bridge because, having become a Christian later in life, I can see things from both sides; the people who aren't Christians and the church.

We do a lot of listening, asking for feedback and trying not to rush in with lots of plans. For example, a few who come to Tea and Toast Church said that standing up when we sang worship songs felt weird. We discussed it as leaders and decided 'yes', it was better to just sit down.

I'm a single mother and my son is autistic and I think overall this has given me empathy; I understand the challenges that parenting brings. When I was a financial adviser, you're quite often discussing confidential issues with people, and that has helped me too. So, I have all these things from my past life which God is using.

I think anybody can plant a church because you don't need to have anything. I had nothing but the heart to have a go. I think that's what I'd like to encourage people with: God will provide anything you need; you just have to have that heart for it. It's a great place to start. It is really good to have a church behind you, like I've had with Locking Castle, because they pray for you and give you practical support, and sometimes financial support.

Sometimes people think church planting is really difficult and you have to do this and that, and be ordained, and go on this course and that course, and I think that can put people off. For me, it was just about having a go, and really a lot of it was about hospitality, which I've always enjoyed. However, I actually felt called to ordination three months after first meeting God.

The first time I went for selection for Church of England ordination, I didn't get through. So I thought, oh well, I'll just get on with life, leading the church. I spoke to the diocese's evangelism team leader Tina Hodgett, whom I'd met very early on in my journey. I told her I was loving my church planting, but I didn't think I'd be going through the BAP[2] again because it didn't work out. But she said to give it another try and pushed me forward. I went through the process again and it was so easy that time! As I went down the pioneer route, the door just flew open, it was the right timing. So, I'm now a curate, ordained as a pioneer minister, and will become a parish priest in summer 2022.

There are 10 of us on our leadership team with different gifts – evangelists, pastors, teachers, practical people, and so

2 A Bishops' Advisory Panel (BAP) makes a recommendation to a bishop about whether a candidate should enter training for ordained ministry in the Church of England.

many more. God has brought people around me who are able to support me, and I've learned lots from them. As people have got involved at the church, they have naturally become leaders, and I've been discipling them, as have others who are more mature. We just spot people's gifts and talents and encourage them in those.

We became a 'conventional district,' a separate entity from Locking Castle Church, in March 2022, which means we're almost like a parish but not quite. We have our own PCC, treasurer etc. There is actually another church in our parish and the vicar there has been supportive. We communicate regularly and are very respectful of each other.

We're in the process of a building project, which is very exciting. Our weekly homegroup was growing and there are only so many people you can fit into a house.

And – we're in the process of a building project, which is very exciting. Our weekly homegroup was growing and there are only so many people you can fit into a house. And the community keeps going on about a community café, because our pop-up café is only once a week. So, we knew we needed to go forward with our own venue. We'd been praying about this for many years and it came to the point where we approached Persimmon, the developers for the new housing estate, with a business plan.

We went to see Persimmon's managing director and shared this vision. He said there was a plot of land available and was talking about a price of £500,000–£600,000. We showed him the plan for a community café downstairs and a mezzanine floor with office space to rent out for different community use and he was very enthusiastic. And then he said we could have this plot – for £1! We were a bit overwhelmed and knew that God must be in it. It's an iconic spot, right in the middle of the development. We can't use it till 2025 because Persimmon are using it for their sales office, but that gives us time to raise the £750,000 needed for the building.

I think the biggest lesson I've learned is to be very prayerful and not rush. It can be quite overwhelming with the building project and all the other stuff, but I'm trying to keep it simple and say every day: 'God, what do you want me to do today?' I don't want to be so busy that I can't stop and chat to people. 'Be still, and know that I am God' is a key verse for me – I've actually had 'Be still' tattooed on my arm!

www.haywoodvillagechurch.org

'In the 10 years since attending The Church Planting Course, God has shown me that with prayer and practical encouragement he enables ordinary people to embrace opportunities for planting and revitalisation and see such exciting growth!'

REVD TOM YACOMENI, Lead Minister, Locking Castle Church

'Church planting has made me feel involved in church in all aspects of community life, every day of the week. It doesn't just feel like something you do on Sunday.'

KATHRYN, Haywood Village Church member

2

SHARON COLLINS

Pop Up Church, Blackburn

*Grandmother Sharon left her home town, moved
to Blackburn, and started an estate church – on an
allotment. She talks about her call, her training, and her
passion for the people with whom she lives and works, on
an estate with significant social challenges but a strong
community spirit.*

I knew I was called to estates ministry when I was doing my
licensed lay minister's training. I'm employed as an urban
evangelist by the Diocese of Blackburn, supported by the Strategic
Development Fund, and I'm attached to the parish church on the
estate, St James Lower Darwen. Coming to Blackburn wasn't a
decision I made lightly – I didn't know the town at all. I was given
a house in quite a tough part of the Roman Road estate and as a
woman on her own, I felt quite vulnerable.

In a way, it helped being completely new here because people
saw I was on my own and were friendly and accepted me. I
didn't know what I was going to do at first, but I didn't think
I was going to plant a church. I wandered into various groups,
like community and crafts groups, and introduced myself to the
staff at the estate management office. I didn't hide the fact that
I'd come to make Jesus known, and after about eight weeks, the
parish vicar said it was time for me to start something. That was
in 2018.

So, I began to think about planting a church and asked people
on the estate, 'What would that look like for you?' A colleague
who's experienced in estates ministry said I needed to make it

clear it was a church and not a social action project, because that's what people were used to. I asked people I'd met on the estate to help shape the church and they got on board pretty quickly.

We started Pop Up Church really slowly, just once a fortnight in the community library, which is run by volunteers. We would put out an anonymous questions box and try to answer the questions together, just sat round a table. The box was really, really popular. There was no worship because how can people sing songs to a God they don't know yet? I would put the *Lancashire Telegraph* on the table and ask people to look through it for things they would like to pray about, things that worried them, or things they wanted to give thanks for. They suggested and I prayed, at the start. Everyone was welcome, of all faiths or none, and word just spread. The grandmothers I'd met brought their children and grandkids.

It grew and grew and then Covid came. The library closed and we were a homeless church. I started prayer-walking in earnest, asking God to give us a space on the estate. From nothing, I was quickly offered four sites, including an abandoned allotment, right at the centre of the estate. We meet under a huge polytunnel. It got slashed, but we raised funds and bought tarpaulins to stitch together to make a canopy. During the winter, we're back in the library, but come the springtime, we'll be in the allotment because it's definitely our spiritual home. I think there's something so important about doing things in public spaces; people are always walking right past, for a start. One guy came in with his daughter because he heard us all laughing! He wouldn't have come in if he'd had to push a door open. I'm not saying all churches should be outside, but it works for us.

I think there's something so important about doing things in public spaces; people are always walking right past, for a start.

My journey began when I fell into a church and did Alpha. Then the vicar invited people he felt had a leadership gifting to devote 10 hours a week to learning about the Bible and sharing food together. After four years, I said I wanted to do something more, so he suggested I did lay ministry training. While I was there, I was asked to co-lead a new congregation called Sofa with the vicar's wife. This was Jill Duff, now Bishop of Lancaster. I started to grow in confidence and co-led other groups, and then was invited onto the senior leadership of St Paul's Widnes, a resourcing church.

I was on the PCC [Parochial Church Council] there, looking at service delivery and outreach mission. I decided to go and 'adopt' a local street and was amazed because the congregation didn't want to get involved. One lady was mad for mission though and together we got this thing going where we just loved all the people on this street, connected with four new families, threw them a barbeque, and it was fab. That spread, and after I'd gone, it went on spreading and the other lady started a prayer group in the next street.

Now I spend a quarter of my time as a tutor for the diocese's training school of urban leadership, M:Power.[1] I'm piloting a daytime M:Power group in Darwen for estate residents who are potential leaders, because people tend to have time on their hands in the day here, not evenings so much. We meet from 10 a.m. to 2 p.m., study the Bible, eat dinner, and then have 'formation' time – discussing things like living as a Christian and our 'hot potatoes,' everyone's questions. The conversations around coffee and dinner are great.

I could see who the emerging leaders were: new to faith but had capability.

I'm a very relational person so straight away I wanted to build a team for Pop Up Church. I could see who the emerging leaders were: new to faith but had capability. Over time, I've discipled these folk and some have come on the M:Power course. Five from Pop Up have just been authorised as lay ministers through M:Power and they're beginning to lead services, do the welcome, and all that kind of thing, to build confidence so that they can develop into mature leaders. Some

1 www.blackburn.anglican.org/m-power-lay-leadership-training-in-urban

have got their own ministries in the workplace or home, inviting people to meet with Jesus.

An absolute highlight for me was our very first baptism and confirmation service in summer 2021, on the allotment. Bishop Jill came along, together with 60 friends and family members of the candidates. We had three children baptised and two adults confirmed. The children's legal guardian is Sarah, who originally came to Pop Up with her mum and really wasn't happy, often interrupting things. But over time, God got to her and she was on her knees in worship, receiving forgiveness. She's now an authorised lay minister for the urban church in Blackburn Diocese! I lived on estates myself; I have a very broken past and Jesus radically changed my life. These are people like me, from my background, meeting Jesus.

My deepest joy has been seeing new people connect with God.

Yes, my deepest joy has been seeing new people connect with God, seeing the changes in them, and hearing them talk about the different choices they've made because of Jesus.

www.facebook.com/romanroadlibrarychurch

'I came to Pop Up as a non-believer to challenge the beliefs of everyone there. God changed me from the inside out and I now have faith and a deep belief in God.'

SARAH, Pop Up Church member

3

DIANE GRANO

Lightwave, Red Lodge, Suffolk

Diane and her team's dynamic approach to mission has reached the heart of a rural Suffolk community. With an 'all hands to the pump' approach, everyone is included and valued in building community and journeying towards a personal relationship with God.

Before I moved to Suffolk, I was a lay member of a parish church team in south London, where my rector Jago Wynne said he wanted to put me forward as an ordained pioneer minister. When I started researching this, a role came up in Red Lodge near Bury St Edmunds, through an Anglican-Methodist Local Ecumenical Partnership. I felt I needed to knock at this door, Jago agreed, and I got the post.

Over the next two years I was based at St Christopher's in Red Lodge, where we had a focus on youthwork, and the youth group really grew, to about 50 young people. Bishop Mike Harrison and Archdeacon Sally Gaze recognised the Lord was at work and issued a BMO,[1] to create three mission hubs in strategic rural areas. They proposed launching the first – called Lightwave – in Red Lodge and I was offered the role of leader, starting in September 2019, just before Covid arrived.

As we consulted with the parish church in Red Lodge, they understandably felt unsettled by the huge investment from the diocese and a BMO in establishing a rural resource church in their parish. Because this was not to be a church plant from St Christopher's, I needed to detach myself from that church

1 Bishops' Mission Order. www.churchofengland.org/resources/parish-reorgan-isation-and-closed-church-buildings/bishops-mission-orders

and start again, without taking people from there into the new expression of church. This was a bit daunting, but I felt that if I believe in Jesus and the fact that I'm his servant, then I must believe this opportunity is from God and for his kingdom, so I didn't find it difficult. Now we are beginning to see collaboration between us and the parish church, recognising that there is place for both, rather than either/or.

We are beginning to see collaboration between us and the parish church, recognising that there is place for both.

Development in Red Lodge started about 10 years ago, from a small truck-stop village. There was a massive new building project, with affordable housing that attracts young families, and families moved by social services out of Essex, Ipswich, and nearby cities with limited space for growth. There are now two primary schools, a few shops, and a sports pavilion, so Red Lodge's amenities support the small villages around.

I spent a lot of time praying and wondering what on earth God was going to do here in Red Lodge. In fact, my take on mission is you pray, listen, respond, have people alongside you – and just start! In some amazing 'God moments,' God gradually brought people to me who are now our core team of six. So we started Lightwave with a breakfast, once a month on Sunday morning, in the sports pavilion. We served good, hot food and it was somewhere to chat, and see if people were even interested in talking about Jesus. We invited people I'd got to know, some from local churches, and it was really 'safe,' no worship or prayer, just a theme on something like forgiveness, which we'd discuss. I'd also share very briefly how, as a Christian, I approached this topic in my own life. This grew and about 30 people came along.

Still being intentional about faith, we began to think what else we could offer the community. There was no social space for people to meet up, so we opened a Saturday morning café too. This was a fantastic gateway to the community, but then Covid hit and everything had to close. We knew that as Christians, the

Lord was asking us to look after those in need, and we wanted to be the light in the darkness for the community. We partnered with the local doctor's surgery, parish council, and county council and became the leading charity on the ground, serving about 12 villages with food and medication.

Covid began to shape the mission and this led to the need for a food bank. The housing developers gave us a shipping container to house one but it was full of concrete and totally unusable. So Dave, one of our core team, and I set-to clearing it out and insulating it. We put in electricity, got some freezers, and launched the food bank. We had a whole operation going: delivering food, spreadsheets, a call centre – which was my home phone – and volunteers taking responsibility for people in dedicated areas. One person's job was to help people register for online shopping. The food bank hadn't been on our radar at all, it just happened, and it raised our profile significantly. I have to say, we were glad when it subsided a bit because it was a lot of work!

The food bank hadn't been on our radar at all, it just happened, and it raised our profile significantly.

Alongside the food bank, we thought hard about how we could grow the café's reach. We decided to run themed events at the café, which would serve different groups of people, and decided on a Thursday morning café for parents and toddlers. We offer entertainment for the kids so we can build relationships with the adults. Faith is quite 'lite touch' here, with some Christian books, among others, for the children, and a kids' Christian song at the end, and there's an open invitation to the Sunday morning 'let's talk about Jesus' breakfast.

Then we realised there's nowhere for teens to be in Red Lodge, unless they can afford to join a sports team, and they end up just hanging around and getting into mischief. So we started a Friday night youth café for Year 6 upwards. We serve a menu that appeals to teens and it's somewhere they can be together – with free food! As well as this social event, we've recently launched the

Hope group for secondary school kids, a place to explore faith, for those who want to stay on for an hour after the café.

And for sports teams and fans, we've got the Saturday morning pop-up café at the pavilion every week. This is an opportunity for people of all ages, from church or community, to volunteer and it creates community and hospitality – and generates some income for Lightwave too. And again, we invite people along to the Sunday morning breakfast, where they can learn more about faith, which is the reason we exist.

Our biggest risk is premises because we're reliant on the sports pavilion, who might need the space we rent at any time. So we're actively looking to collaborate with the Local Ecumenical Partnership and others to build a Christian centre, which we want to be open every day of the week. It's essential that the Church invests in order to grow. With youthwork, the Church is saying 'we want to grow younger,' but how are you going to grow younger? You've got to invest in young people to raise up young Christian leaders.

It's essential that the Church invests in order to grow.

I'm a governor at one of the schools and Lightwave engages with schools, taking assemblies and after-school groups. Up to 80 children came along to our holiday club last year and 25 joined after-school faith groups. We run four big events a year, which requires a massive effort. We organise these centrally and schedule them in four villages in the area, where they don't have capacity to do mission or events but where they love what we do and welcome our support. Invites to the next event go out at everything we run. For example, we organised a Christmas trail family event in Kentford, a nearby village, and gave out invitations to the local church's Christingle service. Because of this, a very old church building that was empty was suddenly full of young families for Christmas! We will keep enabling mission in villages like this, building relationships with people and growing volunteers, and then the Lightwave hub can begin to support other villages, providing the centralised support to plan and publicise events, but not needing to be there in person.

We find it's important for fresh expressions of church who lean heavily into social action to be intentional about moving those entrusted into our care towards becoming mature in Christ, so we started something called Encounter. We meet on three Sundays of the month and have 25–30 people now. It includes worship, a talk, and prayer for each other. We have a really good relationship with St Christopher's, so one Sunday a month we swap venues; we meet in the church building and their congregation gathers in the sports pavilion. We want to show that a variety of forms of worship can exist together and that we're united in building the kingdom. On the other Sunday of the month, instead of a church meeting, Encounter people serve at the Sunday breakfast café, and are encouraged to invite someone along. In two years, we've had five baptisms and confirmations.

I'm still on the path to ordination as this will complete the fullness of the ministry I am called to, which includes offering the Holy Sacraments. I hope to be ordained this summer. Lightwave isn't about me doing everything; I tell the team the kingdom can't grow unless you recognise the gifts in people, give opportunity for them to serve, enable and release them. I think you're doing well as a pioneer if you can take a step back and not exist, otherwise it's all about you. My role is to work in the background and help people to step up into their gifts, Christian or not, because everybody is welcome and because people, in my experience, become Christians through serving and feeling valued. We have about 40 volunteers from the community and different churches all around – we say 'yes' to everybody.

I tell the team the kingdom can't grow unless you recognise the gifts in people, give opportunity for them to serve, enable and release them.

When I was appointed to lead Lightwave, I said to Archdeacon Sally that I couldn't take the role if I was going to be micro-managed. We want to move with the Holy Spirit, and I can't be so boxed in that we can't step into space when the Lord leads. When you spend time with God, you know it's him when he lobs something into your heart, and you just go and do what you sense he's saying. If I first had to ask permission and write a report, we'd still be planning on a blank sheet of paper. If you have a pioneer or church plant, you have to release them fully into all that God intends them to be. And Sally did that, but she also keeps a close eye to support and pray: she talks about 'high accountability, low control,' but it is also about respect and advocacy. I have a regular phone call where she says, 'Di, what wonderful things have you done that I don't know about yet, because I'm about to go into a meeting with the bishop!'

www.lightwavemission.org

'The most inspiring things for me about Lightwave have been seeing new people come to faith, the difference made in the community, and the growth in people's gifts. It is such a privilege to visit Red Lodge and listen to what people say about Lightwave there.

Diane's vocation to begin this work was outstandingly obvious through her character, her values, and her gifts. From her ministry I could see that she was deeply prayerful, incredibly intentional about making disciples, and resilient in the face of difficulties. It also became very clear that God had given us the same vision for making new disciples and already established good local relationships for her to grow a new community. As it happens, I believe Diane is called to ordination – but in this time in her life, the fact that she was not ordained made no difference to the decision to ask her to plant in Red Lodge.'

VEN CANON SALLY GAZE, Archdeacon for Rural Mission, Diocese of St Edmundsbury and Ipswich

'When you've made mistakes like me, nobody will believe in you. But in Lightwave they did. Here they encouraged me to serve and I find I have a lot to give.'

Lightwave member

4

WOLE AGBAJE

IMPRINT, Leicester and London

Still in his 20s, Wole Agbaje has planted churches in Leicester and the City of London. Called IMPRINT, their Gospel Showcase attracts hundreds of young adults and families, who are finding salvation and wholeness through IMPRINT's outreach.

The idea for IMPRINT didn't come from me, it came from a dream I had one night in my second year at Leicester University. I had a dream of something that looked like a production that shared the gospel through creative means. I had the same dream of this event for seven days, back to back. After the seventh night, I woke up and knelt down by the side of the bed and asked God if the dream was from him. And he said to me: 'Yes, it's called IMPRINT and it's a movement that will bring my prodigals back to me.' In 2015 we held our first event, a Gospel Showcase, at the Students' Union. Around 400 young adults came, we shared the gospel, and saw people dedicate their lives to Jesus.

When I felt God saying the Anglican Church was going to be my home, I started crying because I didn't want to be called to the Church of England!

I ended up staying in Leicester when I finished uni, after another dream from God about going to Holy Trinity Leicester, a large city-centre church. This wasn't in my plan, and when I felt God saying the Anglican Church was going to be my home, I started crying because I didn't want to be called to the Church of England! But I knew that's where God was calling me, so I became an intern at the church. We did another Showcase there and 300 students and young adults came. After that, the vicar, John McGinley, told me he felt that God had asked him and his church to support me to start my own church. When my internship finished, Holy Trinity and the Diocese of Leicester gave me their blessing to start IMPRINT Leicester, which launched in 2017.

Around this time, I felt the Lord gave me a word that young adults had become pioneers in faith. I was dragged to church as a child but now young adults are becoming the first person in their household to be saved, so they bring their families along to church. In Leicester, it was mainly students and young adults; in London, it's mainly young professionals, but it's constantly evolving and more families are joining us. I was reluctant to plant in London, let alone move there, but we prayed and discerned as a team that this was the Lord calling. In 2018, we organised our first Gospel Showcase in London and two members of our team moved to the capital to start a small group for city workers. The small group grew, week to week, and they planted a Sunday community a year later. New Wine[1] has given us phenomenal support and gave us a grant towards initial costs when I first moved to London, which really helped me to focus on planting well.

The Gospel Showcase is like a mini West End production – a musical theatre piece, written by our team on a contemporary theme, interwoven with music, dance, poetry, and visual media. I think people want to be entertained and are really surprised by the standard of the production. But it's not just entertainment, each Showcase has a substantial message; we always have a short talk and an altar call. We've seen the Lord set a lot of people free, particularly during the worship and ministry time. At the first Showcase, we weren't expecting this but it's carried on happening and has become integral to what we do. From contacts made at the Gospel Showcase events, we start small groups which can then become a church community.

When we planted in Leicester, we had lots of people on our doorstep and the universities were down the road, but the

1 www.new-wine.org

London plant is near the Bank of England in the City of London, where there are hardly any residents, and we couldn't rely on local people coming. So at least 50 per cent of people came to IMPRINT London through social media or word of mouth. We're just over 200 and have two Sunday services at 2 p.m. and 5 p.m. We run small groups in the City on most evenings during the week, and people come straight from work. We want to have a stronger midweek presence in the daytime, like we do on Sundays, so we're going to start lunchtime services and lunchtime Alpha, hopefully by September 2022.

When I first started in Leicester, I had this belief that because I'd said yes to doing a church plant, I had to carry all the burdens and let everyone else have a good time. So I was preaching but I was also the person setting up the audio system, putting out the chairs, stuff like that and I wouldn't accept any help. I remember I was busy getting the tech set up one day and one of the guys said to me, 'Wole, can I help you?' I said, 'No, no, just carry on chatting to people and I'll do this.' He offered again, and I refused again, and then he said, 'Wole, it's ridiculous that you're the only person in church who knows how to do this!' And when he said that, it just convicted me so much. No one taught me how to church-plant but I realised the way I was approaching it wasn't sustainable. So that's the thing – share responsibilities as quickly as possible. Now I don't worry about the audio equipment! When we came to London, with stuff like stacking chairs after the service, we did it openly and people just wanted to help. It created that culture of 'we do things together.'

The way we've found leaders is quite unconventional, but I rely a lot on prophetic revelation when choosing a team. I can just be praying or walking and God gives me a prophetic picture of a person in a particular leadership role at church. For the most part, it's been a surprise to me when the Lord showed me some people in a particular role, because for some, I didn't know they carried a gift in that area.

It reminds me of when Samuel wanted to anoint the king, and the Lord said to him that humans look at the outward appearance but God looks at the heart. I think in planting, the tendency is to choose people who have tons of experience, who are strategic, but sometimes that's at the cost of choosing the person who the Lord has anointed to do the job. Of course, I run this by members of our team before I approach that person, and we also ask those people to pray, we don't do anything by coercion. It's a crazy thing to ask someone to be in church leadership when they're also in full-time work; it's really costly and they need God's word on it before they do it. We have a big focus on corporate discernment in the team. I try to speak about things really openly and involve our team in decisions about the diocese, finances, and all we do.

The IMPRINT community is just amazing. Oh my goodness, they really love God! They take risks and they serve so diligently and with such humility. My core team of 17 in London are all City workers, all volunteers except for one paid member of staff. They've really got the vision and feel called to it and give their lives to it. Our leader in Leicester is self-funded and works full-time. Seeing people lay down their life for Jesus is just crazy and constantly reiterates to me that it's worth it, even when it's difficult.

Our biggest challenge has definitely been finances. We've often felt that we've been quite under-resourced and we've had to rely on the grace of God and a few people's generosity. Holy Trinity Leicester helped us a lot with a venue and lent us audio equipment, and our connections went a long way; they were almost more valuable than doing it by yourself and having everything.

We grew quickly in Leicester but we didn't always have the resources to match our growth. I think we outgrew five places and ended up with limited resources and no permanent space. I used to have this massive suitcase we called the church planting suitcase, with all our audio equipment in, and we literally wheeled it through the city centre to the next venue. What's really helped in London is having a permanent home at St Edmund the King, right in the heart of the City.

It would have been nice to have an easier journey to this point, but I think it did teach me one of my biggest lessons. The way church planting can be portrayed – and what I thought too – is that you need to have everything – the amazing venue, phenomenal audio equipment, a budget to pay people from the start, and the perfect team. I had none of that! I'm so grateful to God that he was able to build something literally out of nothing. I know now that it is *God* who builds his Church and the best thing we can do is trust and obey him, step by step. I had literally no faith to plant into London. I said to the team – even though we'd had so many prophetic words – we just can't afford London, there's no way. I remember the Lord speaking to me very strongly about it and saying, 'Just because you feel limited doesn't mean I didn't call you to London.' So yeah, the Lord knows what he's doing and we try our best to do what he's saying.

www.weareimprint.org

'By being a part of IMPRINT, I've come to know the value of being in a sound-minded community. IMPRINT has caused me to become more comfortable in sharing both my problems and my wins because the support I've received from this church is that of a family. Through being at IMPRINT, I've come to learn the true meaning of love; biblical, sacrificial, and unconditional love, love that has no limits but looks at the best version of everyone, especially when they fall short of the glory of God. I've made many mistakes, even in church, and yet the love of Christ has covered me and has been available to me not just by Christ but through IMPRINT too. The church has played an integral role in helping me, challenging me, and cultivating me into the man God has called me to be, and for these reasons, among many more, I am so ever grateful for this church, for this community, for this family.'

EDIRI, IMPRINT member

KIMBERLEY LO AND DEREK BAGNALL

Hope4All, Pennywell, Sunderland

St Thomas' Church was on the verge of closing in 2020. But the prayers of the tiny congregation were answered when the diocese came on board and a way for the church to serve local people during the pandemic opened up. Hundreds of people now visit the church every week, where Kimberley and Derek witness them encountering God.

St Thomas' in Pennywell would have absolutely closed a year or two ago, and we are so excited that this wasn't the case. In fact, whenever Kimberley thinks about it, she cries. She was there when there were only about 12 people, faithfully praying with others every week in the Lady Chapel that something would move in our community. Now when we walk into the church, it's at capacity, not one seat left in that café. And everyone is happy and smiling.

It started when Revd Canon David Tomlinson, Director of Strategic Growth for the Diocese of Durham, got in touch with Derek's wife Katherine, who's the vicar of five churches in the area. David persuaded Katherine to look at the Diocese of Sunderland's Communities of Hope (CoH) initiative and she gave the green light to launch something similar in Pennywell, based at St Thomas'. We named our community Hope4All and launched in October 2020.

The first thing we did was open a small food bank, and later, through CoH, a community shop – Shop4All – in April 2021, and

Cafe4All in June. With Shop4All, you pay a £1 membership per month and that gives you access to our food co-op, where all the food is half price or less. It's different to the food bank, because it gives people independence to choose their own shopping and to manage their money. They also get access to two items a week from our sustainability shop, which has clothes, homewares, and toys.

The café is open three times a week, including during Eucharist on a Wednesday. People can see what's going on in the service and join in if they want to. We wanted to show that faith is not alien and God is for everyone – you don't have to be a certain type of person, or be good, to know God. We've introduced a prayer jar so people can write down a prayer need and it gets prayed for at the Eucharist. The person is welcome to come along to the service and that's brought a lot of comfort to people. In turn, the café has really helped people's self-esteem and dignity because buying your own coffee and cake, even at a very low cost, doesn't feel like charity – it feels normal. And everything they pay goes back into the community.

We wanted to show that faith is not alien and God is for everyone.

When people come to the food bank, we always tell them about the shop and the café, so once they're financially a little bit better, the shop can help them along the way. People tell us it's so nice to be able to buy their own food and have choice. It's just brilliant, seeing that. We've now got over 250 Shop4All members. What's happened from that little food bank to here is unbelievable!

In the shop, we do vegetable 'weeks,' like a soup week or a pie week, and have those items on the café menu too, so people can buy the veg and ingredients from the shop to cook the same meal at home. We find people do love to cook, it's just they might not know where to start, cooking from scratch, or they don't have the means or the money, so the shop really helps with that.

At the moment, we just have a small kitchen for toasted sarnies, jacket potatoes, and the like but we now have architect's plans for a proper kitchen, plus an office and training rooms.

We're waiting to hear from the diocesan property team, but hopefully the renovations can start in the next few months. It'll mean we can do proper home cooking for the café and run cookery classes, using the food we have in the shop.

We put all our updates on social media, but we recently did a leaflet drop of about a thousand because the church is on a big estate and not everyone knows about us. Social media is great once you know we're here, but we think the leaflets are essential for getting word out to the community.

Sometimes people comment that the church should be for worship, and we say – this is worship! This is active worship and it's showing people exactly what church is and what it stands for.

Sometimes people comment that the church should be for worship, and we say – this is worship!

By coming here, they're receiving God, and the message that they are loved, valued, and appreciated for who you are. That's the first step to receiving God. We believe in building community first and *showing* people what it's all about, rather than just telling them. People here already show so many Christian values, in the way they look out for each other, have a cuppa together, or give a hug when someone's down, and it's just kind of joining up the dots with them to connect those values with God. We encourage people to get baptised and confirmed, but at the end of the day, that's up to them.

We have a few people who now come to our 'Bible and Cake' on a Monday afternoon, where we focus on some Bible verses, and have coffee and cake of course. Anyone can come along, you don't have to be theologically trained! We talk about God and what we think about the Bible passages – it's not a question of you must think this or that. People who weren't in church before now feel comfortable coming and actually talking about God and the Bible and we think that's because they came through these doors and felt accepted and valued.

During Covid, a lot of things closed, but the church was one of the few things that remained open. People could rely on us and know that we were going to be there. Yes, it was dangerous but God is unchangeable and unmovable, and that's why we felt we must be here. We saw how people built relationships with God, rethinking church, as we helped provide them with whatever they needed, be that company or food or clothes. After the pandemic, when things started to ease off, people felt more free to come into the church and café, and we've continued to welcome them.

For a long time, the Pennywell area struggled, due to loss of industry and jobs locally, and the church had been broken into. Pennywell is now seeing a revival, with industry and new housing coming back into the area. No one has attempted to break into the church, we've got planters outside, and the flowers have been left, not pulled out. We're at the heart of the community now and people have accepted us and appreciate that we are here for them.

We see miracles every day in people. We had to stop someone coming in for a few weeks because of his behaviour but he came back a few weeks later and apologised. He had quite a lot of anger issues and for him to do this was a big deal. We're blown away by the people that we see every day, they're just incredible. These are people who aren't valued in society, but for us, they're *the* most valuable people. We now have people from the community who've offered to volunteer with us and we couldn't do any of it without them.

We have a really good relationship with Revd Canon David, who manages all the CoH projects. We can go to CoH if we need support, advice, or help with funding. We get so much wisdom from David because he's done something similar to Hope4All with Shildon Alive in Co. Durham.[1] He completely understands and gets us.

We feel a lot can be done in the community without ordination.

We're both paid by CoH, Kimberley full-time and Derek three days a week. Neither of us plan to be ordained; we feel a lot can

1 www.shildonalive.org.uk

be done in the community without ordination, and perhaps you can relate to people more easily without it? We're very well supported by many of the local churches too. They come and visit us and use the shop. We get regular donations every week and people will collect food for us as well.

We go by the motto: 'Don't overthink things!' It's just God. Thinking back to how things were before, we can't quite believe all this has happened. What we love about what we do is that if we have a problem, the solution so often just turns up, out of the blue, nothing to do with us. We'll be saying to each other we're running out of something, and then there'll be a knock at the door with someone donating just what we need! God has blessed our church so abundantly that we can't keep up, it's happening so quickly. It's amazing.

www.facebook.com/hope4allcommunity

'I work to ensure that every plant we support is locally owned, shaped, and delivered by the people on the ground who 'get' their place. Kimberley and Derek are a great example of this in action, they are both local Sunderland people who are passionate about the people they live among. For them, the good news of the gospel is a whole of life expression of hope in which no one should be hungry, lonely, forgotten, overtaken by the cares of this world, and so on. Sharing the story of Jesus, the one who carries heavy loads, among people who are oppressed by so much in an easy, relaxed way is something that they excel at. 'Bible and Cake' gatherings, the Mass celebrated while the café is packed, and then picking up the wonderings of those present has just been so beautiful. I delight in their community focus, love of God, and confidence in the gospel.

My role is about prayer, giving confidence, supporting set up, ensuring training and support is in place as required. However, again this too is locally led, I don't impose, I share, inspire, and pray for them. I also look forward to hearing their stories, sharing them on a wider stage, and encouraging others with the possibilities of what could be when God is truly in the room.'

REVD CANON DAVID TOMLINSON, Director of Strategic Growth, Diocese of Durham

6

MARK TATE

The Grove Community, Ealing, West London

Mark has hit both the highs and the lows since launching The Grove Community. Whether it's hundreds of people flocking to community events, or no one turning up to Alpha, he's learning to give it time and prayer as relationships develop and the church becomes a trusted part of this estate community.

We were really, really poor when I was growing up and life was quite challenging. I was brought up in a Christian family and my mum and dad are now both ordained. We lived in a hostel which my parents ran, and I had a lot of friends there, who might be ex-offenders or addicts. We were suddenly made homeless ourselves when the hostel's landlord wanted the property back, and our family had to move into another hostel temporarily. Then we lived on an estate. I didn't realise it at the time, but this all made a big impression on me. I got involved in church in different ways over the years, mainly in a Church of England context, and I had this holy discontent about what wasn't happening. I noticed that the flourishing churches were in the more affluent areas, whereas in poorer areas and estates, the churches were struggling. I felt more and more stirred by this and wanted to see Jesus on our estates.

I noticed that the flourishing churches were in the more affluent areas, whereas in poorer areas and estates, the churches were struggling.

I started praying about this with my wife Laura, and we both felt God calling us to move our family onto an estate. We then spent about two years getting a team together to dream and strategise, preparing one-year, two-year, and five-year plans so we could make starting a church a reality. I was young adults' pastor at St Paul's Ealing at that point, which is in the richest ward in Ealing borough. The Gurnell Grove estate, two miles away, comes in very high on London's social deprivation indices. So it was quite an idea, telling our mates at church that we wanted to plant a church and live on one of the roughest estates in Ealing! We learned that people loved the idea but this didn't materialise into them actually joining the plant.

Over time, we shared what we wanted to do with our local parish church, St Stephen's. They told us they had looked at starting a church on the Grove five years ago, but no one wanted to move there – and they wanted to partner with us. I'm on the leadership team there, and that's where we worship as a family. We're part of each other's DNA and both churches benefit, I'd say. For St Stephen's, partnering with us provides a space for people who have a heart for the community, and hearing stories of transformation builds faith and excitement that God is on the move. For us, we're partly funded by St Stephen's, which we didn't ask for, and which has been an amazing blessing.

I'm a lay church planter and got a Bishops' Mission Order from Bishop Pete Broadbent after Mark Melluish, vicar of St Paul's, affirmed my call to church planting. I've flirted with ordination, as it crops up when you've been in the Church for a while, and though I started the process I have stopped because I didn't feel that call. There's that question of 'will I be taken seriously if I'm not ordained?' so to have that go-ahead from Bishop Pete was really encouraging. We have a board of trustees for the Gurnell Grove Community Trust, a charity we set up in 2017, who are invested in the Grove but separate from the church's leadership team. They're really helpful and keep us accountable.

We launched in 2016 and it was a whirlwind, really challenging. We started with a team of eight people, after six months there were four of us, and after 18 months, just two of us – me and Laura. You kick off and you're all excited by something new but that was quickly shattered by people leaving and saying it wasn't for them. I think the reasons for this were a mixture of people liking the idea of the mission but not the actual reality and cost, Christian immaturity, and also misunderstood expectations. Second time around, I would communicate the expectations and vision as black and white and as early as possible, and get people to commit to this vision together.

On the positive side, this meant we relied on people from the estate much more to help us plant and run the church, and we got to know them a lot quicker. Living here says to people that we're not going anywhere, we're not parachuting in, and they can see how broken we are as Christians. It took about two years for us to really belong here – building trust and acceptance takes a long time. A lot of people know us now and call me when there's trouble, because they don't trust the police. But we now recognise that not everyone has to live on the estate to be involved – which is good, because so far, it's been hard to attract people to move!

Living here says to people that we're not going anywhere.

The week on the estate starts with a community lunch on a Monday, for about eight to 18 people of all ages, who are typically quite isolated. On Wednesday, we run a social group for older people in Heron House, a sheltered housing unit, and in the evening is 'House Church' in our flat. Before Covid, this was quite busy but it's fairly small at the moment, maybe five or six of us. On Thursdays we have a pop-up café, outside in the summer and in the community hall in the winter. That's a mix of everyone, including parents and kids, who have somewhere to play. Friday is our after-school kids' club, and we're about to launch a weekly Sunday service in the community hall. Online stuff doesn't work for us because often people don't have money for the internet. There are four of us on the team: me and Denise, a community worker, who are both supported by funds raised by the Community Trust, and Laura and Paula, who's from the estate. Plus we have about 15 volunteers from local churches who help with all sort of things.

Quite early on, we launched an Alpha course and although 13 people signed up, after a few weeks nobody came. We felt frustrated but we carried on with other community activities and did lots of pop-up events in the first year, like pancake nights and curry nights on the village green at the centre of the estate.

We play bingo, and in the middle we have a short testimony-focused talk and pray for people.

I'd have a big chalkboard and when people came to get their food, I asked them what stuff they'd like to see happening on the estate. Loads of people said bingo! I hadn't done bingo for years since I played it with my nan as a boy. So this developed into 'Bingo Church' once a month. We play bingo – there's no gambling but you can win a fun prize – and in the middle we have a short testimony-focused talk and pray for people. It's been an amazing hit on the estate and we've had lots of fun doing it.

We're an extremely diverse community on the Grove, with lots of people groups. We're probably at least one-quarter Muslim and there are many people with no experience of Christianity, Christians, or church. Some of the older residents have a link to an African-Caribbean church, or Irish families with Catholic connections, and they might go to church at Christmas and Easter. It's quite a cold environment spiritually. People tend to stay in their people groups, so when we've had pop-up community events, it's wonderful seeing all different groups eating and having fun together, because it doesn't happen much otherwise.

We recently had a curry and fireworks night on the estate, to celebrate five years of the church. People cooked curries and the community centre was jammed with 150 people. When we held a Winter Wonderland in 2020 up to 500 people came. People told us they'd never had anything like that before on the estate, just for them. That was really beautiful – we think nice things should happen here because people are special. We go camping once a year, to a Christian festival, which for some is their only holiday.

New things coming up for us are the Sunday service, and a community grocery which we're setting up with The Message

Trust;[1] we have 20 volunteers and we're waiting for agreement from the local council and our MP to release the land to set up a portacabin. People will sign up for a year and get very discounted groceries, twice a week. At House Church, we're starting the New Hope course on trauma, and a Christian psychologist is coming to lead the group in person.

People like Paula are our biggest joy, when you see someone come to faith and start that journey of discovery. We got to know Paula when she came to one of our pop-up events with her kids and really enjoyed it. She is a natural volunteer, so when we started the kids' club, we asked if she'd like to help out. Then she started coming to Bingo Church and brought her friends. Then she came to House Church, which she found quite intense but kept coming to anyway. When we went as a church to a small festival in Somerset, she decided she wanted to take that step of salvation. Two and a half years ago she officially joined the team and it's beautiful, seeing her life transformed. She did the CCX Estates course (now Become),[2] training in estates ministry, which I think is the best around.

People like Paula are our biggest joy, when you see someone come to faith and start that journey of discovery.

So we're praying for more Paulas. We've had a couple of people come to faith but then take a step back. Lots of people have really tough lives here and when something difficult happens, they can't cope. We've got some who are struggling at the moment, and a few on a discipleship journey. I'm naturally someone who likes to take action and see results; it hasn't worked out like that and I've learned to be patient. I've also been reminded we need to pray, especially if you're an 'action person.' We said at the beginning that this is a blank canvas with Jesus at the centre. How we do church is up to us, but we want people on the estate to tell us what they want, rather than for us to come in and say we know

1 www.message.org.uk
2 The Become course, about the Bible and leadership, is designed for anyone who lives on social housing estates or comes from a similar background. www.ccx.org.uk/estates

best. Coming from a large Anglican church, I've had to learn this. Bingo Church is a good example of that. I never thought I'd like bingo, but I love it now!

www.thegrove.community

'Church planting on a local estate has breathed new life into our wider mission to the whole of our parish, and working closely with the new church plant has been a mutually beneficial experience.'
REVD STEVE NEWBOLD, Vicar, St Stephen's Ealing

'The Grove church plant introduced me to Jesus and he has helped bring me out of my shell. I have more confidence and I'm less anxious – I now interact with a lot of my neighbours in our community and help them out where I can, especially some of the elderly folk. It's been a pleasure to help out and be used in this way for God.'
PAULA, The Grove Community member

7

MARY HERVÉ

Thursday Church, Guernsey

'We would never, ever say to someone they are "too bad" to be welcomed and included in Thursday Church,' says Mary Hervé, who pioneered a worshipping community that serves ex-offenders in Guernsey. Mary shares how she and her team celebrate the good while learning to cope with disappointment and creating a safe space for worship.

I have absolutely no doubt whatsoever that this is where God has led me, that it's a calling, even when I've been in very difficult situations. My calling grew organically from when I saw a small advert for help with a prison fellowship service in Guernsey Prison, in 2009. Through that, I got involved with a fortnightly service. Then the prison needed a part-time chaplain, and although, as a school teacher, I had no time to spare, I felt such a strong call to do this. The prison is legally obliged to have a chaplain and although they wanted someone ordained, they took me on a part-time, voluntary basis till they got someone else. Now I work full-time for my church, Holy Trinity, and I'm paid, but remain involved in chaplaincy as a volunteer. Thursday Church, which welcomes ex-offenders as well as others who might be vulnerable and don't feel they fit into mainstream church, is a worshipping community within Holy Trinity.

I have absolutely no doubt whatsoever that this is where God has led me.

Thursday Church began by some ex-offenders coming to an Alpha course at Holy Trinity, who then wanted to continue to meet as a small group. That became a congregation in its own right in 2019. It's a very safe space for people who have started on a faith journey and may have addictions or have come out of prison, after an offence of any sort. We have a number whose offences mean they can't be involved in regular church life because of their licence conditions. Then there's a core of people from Holy Trinity, who turn up regularly and are there to support by their presence. But we don't think of each other in these groups – we're a community, and it's the same deal when people from Thursday Church attend services and events at Holy Trinity.

It's a very safe space for people who have started on a faith journey and may have addictions or have come out of prison.

Back in 2015, I founded the charity Guernsey Caring for Ex-Offenders (GCfEO), which means we get funding for our work. It's an interdenominational Christian charity and my role at Holy Trinity as GCfEO co-ordinator overlaps with my chaplaincy work and Thursday Church. When people attend chapel in prison, it's often their first experience of church and I build up relationships with people, as a chaplain. If they want to come to church when they leave prison, they're invited to Thursday Church. We don't expect people we support through GCfEO to come to church – the vast majority don't.

Most of the people who come to Thursday Church, apart from the team, don't have any previous experience of church. We try new ways to help people take part – like with prayer; we sometimes use a 'prayer ball' to throw to each other, and when you catch it, you pray something simple like 'Thank you God for . . .' At the beginning, we didn't have songs because people found it too embarrassing, but there's one ex-offender who plays guitar well and now when he plays a couple of worship songs, everyone sings heartily.

My biggest joys often come during discussion times – we get into some really deep discussions at Thursday Church. It's when people go, 'Ah – I understand that now!' and you know it's been a light-bulb moment for them. We're talking small numbers, but seeing someone with no church background, who may have committed a serious offence, on a path towards accepting Jesus, is a huge joy. We've had a few baptisms of ex-offenders in the past few years; in fact, someone from Thursday Church asked me just a couple of months ago if they could be baptised.

Obviously safeguarding is a very big issue for us. Everyone who comes to Thursday Church knows there are people within the group whose offences may mean they're on licence, although they don't necessarily know details or who those individuals are. We have ground rules: no one discusses their offences with others; we expect people not to make arrangements to meet outside the group unless they check first if it's appropriate, with myself or my GCfEO colleague Andrew; and the same for swapping phone numbers. For some ex-offenders, we have a church contract in place which is specific to the individual, which they sign. We don't allow anyone under 18 to be part of Thursday Church or be in the building when we're meeting.

At GCfEO, we work extremely closely with statutory agencies, including the police, probation service, Department for Work and Pensions, offender management, mental health services, and third sector organisations. Andrew and I are part of the MAPPA team – Multi Agency Public Protection Arrangement – which manages those with serious offences, such as sex offences, violent crime, and terrorism. So we have this team around us and everything is shared within the confidentiality of the MAPPA group. This overlaps with any serious offenders who are part of Thursday Church, and our vicar, Jon Honour, knows which ex-offenders are under MAPPA. My main safeguarding supports are the police and probation service, which make up the public protection unit, and the diocesan safeguarding lead.

You definitely need support to plant a church, and the type of plant and the people you're serving determines the type of support you need. It's taken a few years to build up credibility outside the church, but when one or two significant people trust you, I find that word spreads. Sometimes we can be frightened of saying we're Christians because we think people will think we're 'do-gooders,' don't know what we're doing, or that we're trying to lure people into our net! But that's generally not what I've experienced. In fact, GCfEO was recently encouraged to apply for funding for a new post by one of the agencies we work with.

I wouldn't have been able to do any of this without the support of my vicar, Jon. He guides me but doesn't micromanage. If I feel I've failed or been taken advantage of, which does happen because of the nature of our work, I know I can turn to him and he will give me time. Team support is vital too: Andrew and I can discuss the nitty-gritty and our volunteers are hugely supportive and practical. Jon is keen on training, so as Holy Trinity staff we do a number of different courses for our development, and more specific training with GCfEO. I'm naturally a risk-taker and Andrew and I are a good balance for each other in that respect. I'm now more careful than I was, but I don't want to lose my ability to take some risks or this work wouldn't happen.

I would say there was a very mixed reaction from the Holy Trinity congregation when we initially launched GCfEO, back in 2015. Most church members were hugely supportive while others expressed concerns. Before Thursday Church began, we'd quite often have people at the Sunday evening service whose behaviour was slightly different, maybe alcohol or drug addicts. So it wasn't unusual for people to turn up a bit the worse for wear or be up and down during the service. Everyone has just become used to it.

Michelle runs workshops that offer practical training, like gardening, arts and crafts, cooking, and furniture upcycling.

GCfEO rents a building opposite the church, where my colleague Michelle runs workshops that offer practical training, like gardening, arts and crafts, cooking, and furniture upcycling. We're about to take on a new member of staff so workshops will now be running Monday to Friday. Some Thursday Church people come to the workshops, and a number of these have progressed to paid employment, which is one of our goals – to help people to get work-ready.

One of our biggest challenges is coping with disappointment. We've had several people who've passed through Thursday Church over the years, excited when they find out about the Christian faith – but then they drift away from church. For me, that's a huge disappointment and I find it hard to understand. But I have to deal with it and carry on, remembering the Bible story of the sower and the different places where the seed falls. We do see one, two, or three whose faith has really blossomed and that gives us so much encouragement. I've learned to rejoice in people's stories, if I can see they've gained something, even if they're only with us for a few weeks.

I never set out to work with the more serious offenders, but they are the ones that people shy away from. Their family and friends have often disowned them, they can't find somewhere to live, either because of their licence conditions or because landlords don't want them, employers may not want them, and they very often find themselves without anybody. We would never, ever say to someone they are 'too bad' to be welcomed and included in Thursday Church.

www.holytrinity.org.gg

'Thursday Church has given more opportunity for ex-offenders and those who support them to build community, worship together, and grow as disciples. This in itself has been a huge encouragement to the four other congregations at Holy Trinity. One of the impacts has been that key leaders in Thursday Church have stepped back from other roles at Holy Trinity, which at first is quite unsettling (what we call the "difficult in-between") but has provided opportunity for new leaders to step up into new roles.'

REVD JON HONOUR, Vicar, Holy Trinity Guernsey

8

PAUL AND JANE ROPER

Trinity Community Church, South Manchester

*Food, friendship, and flexibility have proven key in a
church plant led by Paul and Jane Roper, an accountant
and former teacher. They tell their story of reaching out
to the unreached community on their doorstep.*

Trinity Community Church (TCC) was planted 12 years ago
from a large Manchester church – Holy Trinity Platt, known as
Platt. For years we'd been looking to reach the local area, which
is inner-city. It was a lengthy process, but eventually a group
of people decided to go for it, and we planted a church in a
community centre just 200 yards from Platt! People asked why
base TCC there, but we think being in a community centre is
a really positive thing; it emphasises
that it's a different kind of church,
very much community-based,
rather than being a replica of what
we're doing already at Platt.

*We think being in a
community centre is a
really positive thing;
it emphasises that
it's a different kind
of church, very much
community-based.*

When we started, there were
about 40 of us, and an associate
minister from Platt oversaw us. We
probably spent six to nine months
working out what exactly is church. Is it Sundays? Do we do it
another way? Do we meet midweek at church? All of us together
or shall we have mini groups? We decided to start with two or
three 'mission teams,' which were rather like homegroups but
outward-looking. We didn't have a brief or a template to say what
each must do; it was more, what do you think? Someone was

into football and so they looked at seeing what could happen with that. Jane was involved in a 'knit and natter' group because someone met someone who wanted to learn to knit. And then another person wanted to knit but also learn English, so that turned into a bit of an English conversation group!

We also started Messy Church[1] – and then God sort of hijacked it! An Iranian guy who came to Messy Church was struggling with his marriage and he ended up living with us for a while. He became a Christian and invited his Iranian asylum seeker friends to church, and within a couple of years we realised our ministry was to Iranians, primarily. The original vision was that we would be reaching out to the local white working-class population, but that didn't really happen – the Iranians were becoming Christians and we thought, we've just got to go where God is leading us.

We thought, we've just got to go where God is leading us.

About six years ago, the church had become too big to be a close community so we divided into two. This was the point at which we took on the role of congregational leaders, in addition to Paul's job as an accountant. Before the church plant, we'd led services and been involved in the youthwork, led a homegroup and overseen a cluster of homegroups. So we've had leadership opportunities and also training input over the years. The way it's worked out is that the 'other half' – TCC Rusholme – are mainly the Farsi-speaking Iranian group, and are also linked to Kurdish ministry. At 'our half' – TCC Fallowfield – we're probably now doing more like what we set out to do in the first place, reaching the mainly white working-class population, along with many other ethnic groups. We meet in a volunteer-run library, which has been great. They are pleased with the income we provide and we love our relationship with them and think the location is fantastic, and because it's a place that local people know, they are happy to come in.

We reckon we have about 11 different 'heart languages' at Trinity Community Church. We primarily use Arabic, Amharic,

1 www.messychurch.org.uk

and English. When we have something on the screen in church, we have it in these three languages and we often use images as well. We use the New International Reader's Version of the Bible because it's simple, and we encourage people leading the service to use simple English too. This works for everyone, because whatever your language, some people struggle to read and understand English.

Platt would call itself conservative evangelical but we're not sure TCC really has a label. If anything, we just call ourselves a church plant. A lot of what we do is about relationship. We've found that relationships with asylum seekers build very quickly because they're in a vulnerable position and keen to make contacts. With local people, it's a much slower burn, so it's about meeting people where they're at and building those relationships.

A lot of what we do is about relationship.

Our biggest joys are people, like James. When the weather's nice, we try to offer refreshments outside on a Sunday because there are often people walking past. James was local, and he stopped for a drink and just stayed. He was one of those guys who made friends with everyone, and he was soon telling everybody about his church. He was missing from church for a few weeks, and he told us he had a brain tumour that was terminal. Through this, it was such a privilege to be welcomed into his family. James' father had died only a year before and the family wanted to do something to commemorate their father while James was still alive. So they asked us to do a thanksgiving service, and within lockdown restrictions, many of the family and friends came along. It was such a privilege to do that, and sadly, when James died, we took his funeral as well. We felt we were in that place as part of God's plan for James' spiritual destiny.

One thing that's challenging about planting is keeping the initial vision alive. We're not here for ourselves but to look outwards, and it's easy to drift back into being a nice comfy church and lose that edge. It can be hard keeping everybody on board. We're trying to have a Sunday every year when we say this is what we're about as a church, and hopefully the more you bang on about it, the more people will get it. It's about people knowing everything isn't organised, they can just turn up; it's actually more about everybody getting stuck in.

We're linked to Platt and our finances go through them, but they don't have financial input into TCC. We pay towards the Platt curate's salary, who oversees us and has responsibility for us. TCC's vision is to plant again from our two planted churches, hopefully with a group of people from Platt too. It takes a long time to grow leaders, so if you divide a church every four or five years you end up with a lighter and lighter leadership group in each plant, and managing that is tricky. So taking people from each plant is better. At the moment, we're grappling with this and how we train leaders practically. The danger is thinking we can just send people on a course, but you need hands-on experience as well.

Key for us is having people who aren't working full-time who can use their spare time to do church stuff. So Jane, a former teacher, is one of a few who intentionally don't do full-time work. Our midweek groups couldn't run otherwise. Something else we've really valued is people who have a pastoral heart, so it's not the congregational leaders doing all the pastoring. That's something we've encouraged.

Second time around, we think we'd want to start with a clearer idea of what we want. We'd know what we're about and how we want to do it and we would make sure everyone knows that. There are two kinds of plants: the franchise model, doing exactly the same kind of thing as before, and the ones that are more organic and flexible, which is us.

Do we ever doubt our call? Frequently! Paul's great at saying 'we believe God's called us to this so until he stops calling, we're here.' If you want to plant, we'd definitely say do it. We were aware of feeling comfortable in our church situation and planting forced us to depend on God much more. You know you haven't got the resources, so you do see God at work. The most important thing is prayer, but it's so easy for it to slip off the radar. We've explored praying through a passage of Scripture, with no particular agenda, and spending time focussing on God, rather than just bringing a load of requests before him.

Our other top tips would be these: Firstly, be flexible. One of the advantages of a small church is that you can react very quickly. For instance, when lockdown happened, we went to Zoom straight away and there were no issues. That's a good thing but can be a challenge because some people like things much more organised and find it hard if things don't pan out the way they expect. Secondly, keep the vision: don't lose sight of what you're planting for. Thirdly, and this sounds a silly thing but isn't, spend time eating together. So much of what we do is centred around food, partly because it's a way in which most people, from every culture, whatever their circumstance or background, feel they can contribute. It's so important, both in small groups and together as a whole church.

www.plattchurch.org/who-we-are/tcc

9

ANDY WILSON

Share Matson, Gloucester

Sharing life together is the heartbeat of a new Gloucester fellowship. Church Army leader Andy Wilson unpacks the new approach and new friendships that have brought fresh hope through 'Share Matson.'

Share Matson started in August 2019, seven months before the first lockdown. Matson is an urban area on the edge of Gloucester – our claim to fame is the nearby dry ski slope where Eddie the Eagle trained! I'd describe us as a pioneering worshipping community, rather than a church plant, because plant implies we've come from somewhere, like a sending local church, whereas we – my wife Emma, our daughter Grace, and I – started Share Matson from absolute scratch.

I'm a licensed lay minister, paid by the Church Army. I realised I had a passion for people who were not engaged with church when I was writing a dissertation on missional communities for my master's degree. Initially I felt a call to work with youth, but that grew and got wider and wider and soon I wanted to tell everyone they were loved and valued by Jesus, and to find that sense of community with others. I worked in a pioneering setting in Harrogate and then the Church Army asked me to look at this post in Gloucester. They wanted to pioneer because the local parish church, which is a long way from much of the housing, had dwindled to about five or six people. There hadn't really been much engagement between the church and the local community. Matson comes in very high on social deprivation indices and it's quite a tough place to live, in terms of employment, education, income etc. People can be quite reactive and angry and I think that's partly because, over the years, a lot of things have been 'done to' Matson rather than journeying with the people who live here. But there is an immense sense of community and people know each other well. We're called Share Matson because right from the start I loved the idea of sharing a journey together, sharing life, questions, and meals.

We're called Share Matson because right from the start I loved the idea of sharing a journey together, sharing life, questions, and meals.

At the beginning, I spent two or three months prayer-walking and listening to God, rather than 'doing something' straight away. It took me about 18 months to really understand what I was encountering in Matson, the undercurrents if you like. A couple of months in, I felt a growing link to the Old Testament leaders, like Daniel and Nehemiah, and the value of serving the community. They served, and out of that, were honoured by the community, and then had influence in that community. That's what we set out to do – serve the community in different ways.

So there are about 25 of us now and all but two people had no real church background before. We're largely white, reflecting the local population, with ages ranging from eight to about 60. Monday to Thursday, we have a digital 'thought for the day' live on our Facebook page, with a monthly theme, and on Tuesday and Thursday evenings, we meet as a group online and do games and fun stuff together. On the Thursday, we summarise the week's content, with space for asking questions and sharing thoughts. On alternate Sunday evenings, we eat together at a local church hall at the centre of the estate and have time for discussion about the week's theme. On the other Sunday, we're live on Facebook. Being digital grew out of the pandemic, but a lot of people here have family and health issues and actually find it easier to meet online. We also host a weekly Bible study for two or three people who asked for this.

A year ago, we developed a vision for a café on the estate and we've set this up in partnership with The Long Table,[1] a food-based action group in Stroud. It's open 8 a.m. to 2 p.m. Monday to Thursday at the hall, and it's a hub for meeting and chatting about life. It's very relationship-based, sharing life together and having a coffee. My wife Emma took a massive leap of faith last year and gave up her job at Homebase to lead the café, which is on a 'pay as you feel' basis. We have a play area for kids and a clothes swap rail. A couple of people volunteer with Emma – they said they don't want to be paid, they just want to help because they think the café is amazing.

What people have shared with us through the friendships made has been astonishing. This is one of my biggest joys and we feel really humbled by the trust people place in us. I had a bad cold around Christmas time and was starting 2022 feeling rather ill and de-energised. Just after New Year, someone in our community knocked on the door and gave me a gift. It was a glass, engraved with a message: 'Andy, you are dad to our extended family.' Truly all we've done is spend time with people – we value them and their story, we pay attention to them and their lives. People come to us when they're struggling because they know we won't talk about them behind their backs.

What people have shared with us through the friendships made has been astonishing.

Gloucester Diocese is very encouraging. They're very aware it's not easy pioneering in this context and they take a long-term view. They've said many times that it's a marathon, not a sprint. The bishops and diocesan teams have demonstrated openness and relationship all the way through and I've always had people to talk to when I have had struggles. When I went through a rough patch due to stress, the diocese got me help that day. I can go to the Church Army too, who have been amazing, and two vicars whose churches are close to Matson have really championed me and encouraged me.

1 www.thelongtableonline.com

I'd been praying a lot about developing new leaders and three names kept coming to mind. I was saying to God, 'It can't be these three because I'm not sure where they are in their faith.' Anyway, I asked Bishop Robert [Springett] to come and meet our community, and he was keen to visit us. I invited everyone from Share Matson to come along to the hall and meet Bishop Robert, while privately praying, a bit unusually, that whoever turned up I would invite to be leaders and do team together. The only people who showed up were those three! So I thought, 'OK Andy, that's definitely God giving you a nudge!' Amazingly, they all agreed, saying no one had ever asked them to do anything like this, and they weren't sure what they could bring but they wanted to bring it. They are starting out in faith and learning as they lead.

The thing I'm really passionate about is being community, and when you get to about 25–30 people, I think you start to lose that sense of community a bit. So we're looking to see how we can multiply two or three communities in the next few years, train up local leaders, and then maybe my role will be training those leaders. I'm an extrovert and it's easy for people to gravitate to me, but I want us to grow so it becomes less and less about what I'm doing, so if I leave or retire, it won't all collapse.

For those sending others out to pioneer, I would say: don't send people out alone but in twos, at least, the way Jesus did it, because it's a more healthy way; allow space and time for them to check and confirm their calling in that community; when underway, give them as much time as possible without pressures and expectations; recognise and champion them, with committed support, and – really key – be aware of the need to support that person's family. When I meet with my Church Army line manager, almost the first question they ask me is: 'How are Emma and Grace?'

My advice for someone thinking about pioneering would be: make sure you feel called, not because others think it's right for you or there's nothing else on offer; observe all the factors that are affecting life in your community, as well as listening to people; have a robust network of supporters, who cheer you on and pray for you, and others to be accountable to, who you trust to ask the tough questions; and finally, don't stop learning, from books, podcasts, webinars – feed yourself so you can feed others.

www.facebook.com/matsonshare

'The establishment of a Church Army Centre of Mission led by a lay pioneer minister was a clear part of our strategy both for the renewal of the church in a particular community and to develop the culture of ministry in our diocese so that lay and ordained, of equal value and importance yet with different callings, were seen as able to work creatively together to share the love of God and for the coming of the kingdom.

It has been so good to work with Andy in this ministry. As a lay person his presence reminds us that the call to share the love of God in Jesus Christ is one that properly belongs to us all, and his deeply incarnational ministry in the community reflects the love of God who comes to dwell with us in the stuff of every day.

It's a journey as we seek to form what is authentically church with word and sacrament being Christ's presence, but what a journey with Andy's joy, enthusiasm, and delight in people discovering faith and being formed into community encouraging us all.

It is a privilege to share in ministry with him.'
RT REVD ROBERT SPRINGETT, Bishop of Tewkesbury

'Whenever I have tried to join churches or Christian groups before, I have always felt like the odd one out. Never unwelcome, but it's like I don't fit the mould of what a Christian should be. But since finding Share Matson, I feel that I belong, and am where I should be at the right time.'
VICKY, Share Matson member

10

BERNICE HARDIE

WAVE Church, North London

When Bernice couldn't find an inclusive worship setting for her daughter to join, she and some friends started their own group. Everyone wins when everyone is included, says Bernice, whose WAVE model is inspiring others.

We're not a church and we're not a plant. I guess we're more like a seed. When you say you're a church, it raises expectations of doing certain things in certain ways. We don't tick all the boxes, but we never intended to. My journey started when my daughter, who has Down's Syndrome, was an adolescent. A group of us, either parents or people professionally involved with disability, were looking for ways to make church accessible for our young adults with disabilities. Most of us were part of St James Muswell Hill.

We needed an accessible building suited to the sort of informal services we wanted to put on, where we could serve tea and coffee and cake at the end and people could move about and chat. We couldn't do that at St James because of a timing clash. So we found a home at the local Methodist church, who'd just done a huge refurb of their building, specifically because they wanted to make it more accessible. We went with our church's understanding, and our hope was that not meeting in our parish church gave the message that all denominations were welcome.

WAVE – We're All Valued Equally.

We started WAVE – We're All Valued Equally – with about 12 people, through word of mouth. Now we're about 40. We meet once a month and a typical service is co-led by someone with and someone without a disability. Structure and familiarity are very important: we start with a couple of slides about WAVE, a welcome, and sing the same songs each time, using Makaton signing. We'll have an interactive activity, like a drama or game, then preaching with a visual element. We have tea and coffee and homemade cakes at the end, which for some is the highlight of the afternoon!

When you're part of inclusive worship with people with learning disabilities, there's a tangible sense of the Holy Spirit there, of being closer to the heart of God. It's something about people's openness and trust and joy. I think it's the joy that is deepest. We recently had some visitors from Darlington who are interested in the WAVE approach and they said they were so glad they'd come in person because it was the sense of joy that they felt most.

St James has been encouraging and supportive, and we come under their safeguarding, as a recognised new Christian community. I think their main support is allowing us to use their space for free, like when we started WAVE Club, two years in. This was a social club for people with and without learning disabilities, and was inspired by our original vision, which was very much about church and community coming together. This has now morphed into a regular pop-up arts café event at the local United Reformed Church.

WAVE Club, a social club for people with and without learning disabilities, was inspired by our original vision, which was very much about church and community coming together.

Disability isn't cool, in the way some new church communities are seen, and I think the importance of inclusive worship is often overlooked. Disability initiatives tend to be run by women and I think there is a bias in the Church, giving greater attention to initiatives that involve white, well-spoken men. We are working with families who live with huge challenges and it feels unfair that it is mainly parents who are left to start and sustain the inclusive services needed in the Church. It's great to get encouragement and we've had really encouraging messages from Bishop Sarah [Mullally]. But what I would love is for inclusion to be part of theological training, seen as having as much value as learning Greek, and perhaps for ordinands to have a placement, even just one term, with disability congregations. To me, inclusion is a bit like making batter: you start with the egg in the middle and other ingredients around, and as you gradually mix them and reach out and out, they blend.

When we started WAVE, I had no experience of church leadership and didn't feel equipped at all! I'd been in church all my life, to some degree or other, and I'd helped to lead a pastorate and meetings, but being a church warden at St James was the closest I had come to understanding how the church works. What helped me most was having words of affirmation from people, people of faith who I respected. I had a lot of time on retreat which really encouraged me, because there were many moments of doubt when I asked, 'Why am I doing this!'

When we started WAVE, I had no experience of church leadership and didn't feel equipped at all!

I have an amazing team of people around me and that's what has made the difference between us being able to carry on or not. Most of us have family members with learning disabilities, or some professional connection. The team are really good at making sure people who come to WAVE Church feel welcomed and accepted.

In fact, it has been amazing how God has brought along the people we need. We were very lucky when we started in having a former SEN [Special Educational Needs] teacher who had run a Messy Church, so she had some really practical skills and ensured we had safeguarding elements in place. We have people who are good at tech, and a very talented musician to lead our worship, and we've got people like Sally, who comes and clears up. She does all the washing-up and is always the last to leave.

Then there are the people who pray, like Maureen, a lady in her 70s, who was an absolute prayer warrior when we started. I think she kept me sane in those first couple of years.

I would say to anyone starting out on planting: be very clear who you are planting for. We had a very clear sense of who we were looking to serve. Get your team and make sure you have those who believe in the power of prayer and will have your back in praying. It's helpful to have a bit of training, but we learned as we went along. We made mistakes but people were very forgiving because they were glad that at least we were trying. At one point, people with younger children wanted to come and I had to say no, because WAVE is specifically for adults with learning disabilities. I think it makes life easier if you're absolutely clear who you're for and who you're not going to try to stretch yourself to accommodate.

Another important thing to say is that although, when we started, we were doing this for individuals and families with learning disabilities, we found that everyone who came was benefiting. We realised we were doing things *with* and not *for* each other. That's when we made sure there were always people with learning disabilities, as far as possible, involved in every level of the meeting, from leading to praying and reading.

I continued to work as a market research consultant until two years ago. I was getting really squeezed with work and WAVE and so I decided to give WAVE a year – now two years – full-time, but unpaid. We became a charity in 2020, specifically with the goal of encouraging and equipping others to start inclusive places of worship. I'm really excited to be part of Cinnamon Network's Incubator programme,[1] advising and supporting church-based initiatives who want to set up something like WAVE. This is happening in other areas of North London as people see the need in their community and find the courage to think, 'We can do this.'

I said at the start that we're not a church plant, but people have come to WAVE and said, 'This is church.' After Covid, after

1 www.cinnamonnetwork.co.uk/cinnamon-project-incubator

meeting online, it was just magical seeing people in person and engaging with one another, and I thought, yes, we are church. It's not about being in a building doing things in a particular ecclesiastical way, it's about people loving and caring and supporting each other, and loving Jesus as best they can while they do that.

www.waveforchange.org.uk

> '*I have to say, sadly and truthfully, that at almost every church my son Rob has been treated like a terrible burden. Praise God, he led us to this small diverse church where Rob was loved just like everyone else.*'
>
> ALISON, WAVE Church member

1 1

EMMA MILES

West Hill Community with St Mark's, Bridlington

Emma knows what it's like to 'wake up and wish you hadn't.' She is passionate about sharing Jesus' hope with the neighbourhood where she grew up, in a space that welcomes everyone and speaks the language of the community.

I'm from Bridlington in Yorkshire and I grew up on the West Hill estate. There's a history of substance abuse and a lot of fear and anxiety in my family. At 18, I moved to London – I was really running away from my life on West Hill. I was a recreational drug user and thought you could choose to become an addict or not, but unfortunately the two things go hand in hand, so by the age of 23, I was on Class A drugs, and by 26, I was in my first rehab.

My mum very rarely contacted me in rehab subsequently, but that first time, she sent me a letter that said: 'You know I said there isn't a God? Well, I was wrong, there is, and his name is Jesus. Give your life to him and he will heal you from heroin addiction.' I remember that really penetrated me, right at that moment. I went to call my mum on the centre's phone but the line was engaged. While I was waiting, a book on a shelf nearby jumped out at me – *Chasing the Dragon* by Jackie Pullinger. I remember reading the back cover and Jackie wrote exactly the same thing as my mum had said: she had found a cure for heroin addiction and it was the Holy Spirit.

I was still addicted and broken but left rehab early and went back to Yorkshire. I discovered I was pregnant at the same time

I gave my life to Jesus. I definitely felt the presence of God in my life – I didn't know what it was but I knew something had happened. I was lying in bed with my daughter Faith one day and in that moment, in my bedroom, I was baptised in the Holy Spirit. I didn't ask for it, it just happened. Love and mercy flooded me. I remember just sitting there and crying and saying, 'How can you love me this much?'

You'd think that would be the beginning of an amazing journey, and while I always knew 100 per cent that Jesus was the answer to my problems, I wasn't strong enough to stand, and I had my feet in both camps. By the time my daughter was 18 months, I was back, fully immersed in addiction, only this time, I hit new lows. Social services removed Faith when she was nine and put her into my mum's care.

I remember this was a light-bulb moment; I knew I was being given a choice between life and death and I knew I had to go to rehab. I went to a Teen Challenge rehab centre for 18 months and that's where the journey began to this life I have now – that was eight years ago. Teen Challenge put deep principles into my life: discipleship, accountability, how to beat temptation. All this has stayed with me and been really valuable – this is the foundation for the leadership that I have now.

God spoke to me a lot towards the end of my time in rehab and I had a strong sense that I wanted to serve in any capacity, so I started volunteering at a church. I then worked in care for the elderly for three years, and while I was there, I saw an opportunity to bring Jesus into the care home. There is a statutory requirement for care homes to meet spiritual needs, and this one wasn't doing that. So I started a fellowship group, which had about 24 residents, plus staff and families. Revd Mark Carey, vicar of Christ Church Bridlington, said to me, 'You've started a church!' I hadn't thought about it like that, but yes, it was a

God spoke to me a lot towards the end of my time in rehab and I had a strong sense that I wanted to serve in any capacity, so I started volunteering at a church.

church. And it was a stepping stone into the work I was then offered.

Mark had just arrived as vicar at that point and spoke to me about a potential job. The existing church on West Hill estate was desperate for someone on the ground to do mission. So in 2019, I was employed by Multiply, the Diocese of York's pioneering ministry.[1] I worked full-time, half with West Hill, on community development, and half with Christ Church, who wanted me to work with restoration of broken lives, particularly people with addictions.

When I started, I used to just walk the streets of West Hill on my own. I had so many memories of each street, from being there as a child. As I walked, I would speak out loud the words from Isaiah 60:1 over the estate: 'The glory of the Lord is risen over West Hill.' And I would pray: 'Show me where you're already working.' Ongoing, this is how it's been: God has led my every step and I've just responded to him. One of the biggest lessons I've learned is the importance of prayer, and I think it started here, praying in the streets.

This is how it's been: God has led my every step and I've just responded to him.

As well as my prayer walks, I knew I must get to know people's names and start to build relationships. There was no great spiritual instruction – just to love the estate. So we – a small team of women, including my sister – started Turning Up, where we could worship together and pray for each other on the estate, and we ran a Bible discovery group.

When the pandemic hit, West Hill Church closed. I was in and out of the building lots to use the freezer as we were helping families with meals. Every time I walked through the church hall, I had memories of being there as a child, of community and laughter and families, but the recent memories I had of the church – well, it was almost like I felt I couldn't go back to the old way of doing things. I kept thinking 'what is this?' and began questioning if I'd been called to the estate after all. Eventually I

1 www.multiplyreach.org

spoke to Mark and he said, 'Well, maybe God doesn't want you to go back. Maybe it is time to plant something.'

That began stirring something in me. Perhaps we could start something that would speak the language of the community? The role I had with Multiply was about identifying people aged 20–40, who have very little church background. I knew they wouldn't 'get' the traditional stuff of church, and I didn't feel confident even inviting people into a service. I wanted to create home, where people could come in; not about 'us' running a church and then 'you' strangers coming in, but it being your space. It's meeting people where they're at, who may not have a clue about church culture and language. In my experience, the Church isn't always so good at that.

It's meeting people where they're at, who may not have a clue about church culture and language.

So our first real event was in September 2020 during lockdown and it has been a rollercoaster of a ride. We started with Facebook live and we had about 18 families with us. We'd send out packs made up by volunteers, with a Bible story for the week, family activity based on that story, a treat, things like that. So one week, when we looked at Matthew 6:25–27 – 'Look at the birds of the air; they do not sow or reap or store away in barns, and yet your heavenly Father feeds them' – we sent out bagel birdfeeder kits and asked people to upload photos of their birdfeeder in action. Then around January 2021, when we could meet outside, we started a Saturday morning meeting in Christ Church's garden. We'd have a picnic, usually about 12 of us, and then split into groups and look at a Bible story, asking questions about what God is saying in this passage and how it applies to us. The following week, we'd ask what difference that had made to us.

When we got to the summer, we wanted summer holiday Saturdays to be about the wider community, inviting people in. We'd get ready with a circle of prayer, then fire up the pizza ovens and have loud worship music blasting out. It was fantastic! We had so many families come along.

During the winter season, we meet on Thursdays. We start 'Love West Hill' with prayer and breakfast, then watch *The Chosen* [a TV biblical drama] together. Later in the day, we get food ready for our gathering at 4 p.m., which I have to tell you is absolutely crazy! We have about 15–30 adults and 20+ children. I try to have both loud and quiet times in the meeting, so we have games for the kids to run about and worship where they can jump around, and quiet moments are a 10-minute craft session and a short Bible talk. We always end up in a 'circle of thanks' and we always eat together. Food is really important, I think because it's what real families do, and it brings people together. Jesus often seemed to be sitting with others, eating. Sometimes it's quite hard to see where God is working, with kids charging around and people looking at their phones. What's lovely is that people get involved with clearing up and the washing-up and just naturally take responsibility for things.

So that is church, and then discipleship is happening on a one-to-one basis. We're investing in three people at the moment and that is giving me such joy. Three leaders meet with three people. One is Michelle, who I've known for 16 years – we lived on the same street. For a long time, she came along to things but had no real interest in Jesus, but she's had quite a journey recently. Feeling broken and at the end of herself, she said she'd been watching me and how my life had changed, and she wanted to learn about God, so I'm walking with her and praying with her. I have a level of compassion for people because I know what it's like to be in utter darkness; to wake up and wish you hadn't. I can really identify with that and can be totally straight with people – I have authority to speak because I've been there.

I know what it's like to be in utter darkness; to wake up and wish you hadn't. I can really identify with that and can be totally straight with people.

I haven't had formal training. Teen Challenge gave me a wide range of teaching and I also have training opportunities via the diocesan Multiply programme. I couldn't do this without support on the ground from Christ Church's leadership and my team. Mark is very good at giving on the spot support and teaching. He doesn't try to control but wants me to learn and be confident that I'm hearing God for myself. He gives me permission to fail and grow through that. I'm accountable to others for things in my life and I bring everything to my leaders.

God is at work on the estate and I need to be listening to him, be a willing, prayerful vessel, and turn up. We lost people from church after the pandemic, which was disappointing, but God quickly challenged that disappointment. He brought others from the estate, and that's why we are there. I used to live in desperation and it pains me that people are living in such hopelessness on the estate. I know the life I get with Jesus and I want to see people set free and become disciples themselves. This is what I have a passion for.

www.facebook.com/welovewesthill

> 'Church planting is important to me as a vicar because it keeps me focussed on evangelism and not just running a church. It awakens us to the need people around us have of a relationship with God and renews our vision for mission across our parishes.
>
> We entrust church planting to lay leaders because they are already connected to those they are sent to. They have a sense of people and place that connects with a calling to do something with God.'
>
> REVD MARK CAREY, Vicar, Christ Church Bridlington with Bessingby and Ulrome

'I have seen him change lives, now I want God to change mine. I have also seen the peace and safe place they have found in him. This pulls me in and I want some of that.

What I most love about being a part of West Hill Community is the love and the friendships I have made, how we all care about one another, and no matter what your background, you're always welcome. We are all one big family, God's family.

The biggest thing I have learnt about God so far is his love, how he is always patient, and how, all my life, he has been faithful without me even knowing it. This makes me feel safe and loved and I never feel alone, something I've not really felt throughout my life. I also feel a peace inside of me, and that no matter who we are or what we have done, there's no judgement – he loves us all.

I love being a part of the church community. I have so much more to learn but I already feel so full of hope.'

MICHELLE, West Hill Community member

12

SARAH SHARPE

Connect Gamston, West Bridgford

Launching Connect Gamston in a local school was a slow burn over many years for leader Sarah Sharpe. Looking back, Sarah sees how God was training and equipping her to lead a new worshipping community – even if at first she had to hide her dreams from her husband.

I grew up on the edge of Gamston, watching the new houses being built in the 1990s. We used to play in the fields around here and I came to St Luke's – now my sending church – with a friend when I was a child, just as something to do on a Sunday. I became a Christian in 2004, through the Alpha course at St Luke's, and then volunteered at the church for a couple of years before I became their paid youth worker for four further years. This led to a move in 2010 to Knowle Parish Church in Birmingham, which was a real step-up, really key for me – I was managing other staff and a 40-strong group of volunteers.

I began to feel I knew youthwork so well I was getting a bit lazy about relying on God. At that point, my family and I had moved back to West Bridgford and St Luke's was looking for someone to fill in as children and families minister. I got the job and really had to lean on God because I knew nothing, although I had related skills and knew how church worked. After about a year, the vicar Mark Fraser said they wanted to make my post permanent and I could either concentrate on children and families, or split the role alongside planting a church in the Church of England School in Gamston.

Choosing to plant in the school was something that had been talked and prayed about for 10 years. It's the logical choice because the St Luke's building is just outside the estate, whereas the school is right at the centre, and it's within St Luke's parish boundary. It's a nice estate with mainly detached houses, and a small area of social housing.

Choosing to plant in the school was something that had been talked and prayed about for 10 years.

My husband John was adamant he didn't want to be part of the plant because we'd just moved back to St Luke's from Knowle. I remember being on holiday and I'd taken a book on church planting, but I hid it in my wash bag and only read it in secret on the loo! Taking the job had big implications for my family, with me having to work on a Sunday. But gradually John softened to the idea, at first saying he was happy for me to go and him to stay at St Luke's and then wanting to come on board himself.

So I opted for the St Luke's split role with the church plant. Mark suggested I get a team together and start exploring the vision for this plant. I was quite clear that I shouldn't engineer who should be on the team because I might well be surprised by the people who would be part of it. I waited to see who would come forward and gradually a team of 10 emerged. One couple, Nathan and Victoria, were invited to join almost in error, because of a confusion between this team and a small group! But it was definitely a God thing that they came in as leaders. The team is a real mix of people and ages, lots are key workers, like doctors and teachers.

We didn't know how to plant a church so we had to be very reliant on God and I tried to stop us rushing ahead with man-made plans. We got together every week from September 2018, to pray, talk, share testimonies, get some training from the diocese, and make sure we heard one another's thoughts and ideas. We didn't get anything concrete down on paper until March 2019. It's in my nature to rush ahead but I really felt God was putting the brakes on so we could spend time like this. I know the area really, really well but felt we mustn't assume, must listen to people, wait, watch, and pray a lot. I think it was a bit frustrating for some of the team, but it really paid off.

In this period, we ran two focus groups, where we invited people from the community to tell us what they loved about Gamston and the area, and what they would want from a new church. It was really great because they were reflecting back to us some of the values we felt were important. Encouraging people to be a participatory church, not passive, was key and one man,

We invited people from the community to tell us what they loved about Gamston and the area, and what they would want from a new church.

not a churchgoer at all, said that if he went into a church and saw chairs all in a row, he would feel he had to conform and fit in, whereas if everyone pitches in and puts the chairs out as part of the service, he would feel part of it right away. As we have a huge set-up each week and no storage in the school hall, this was great to hear! And that value has really become embedded in the church; no one would think of rushing off without helping to clear up.

In 2018 we ran a parenting course in the school, and then a parenting teens course. These were really popular and a lot of people from outside the church came along. We launched our Sunday afternoon service in September 2019. Now we probably have 50–60 regulars, and weirdly, always 95 people at our big events, like Christmas! We alternate intergenerational services, when Connect Kids are part of the service, with kids meeting separately, when the adults have worship with just one guitar and time to chat. During the week, we also run Alpha, are involved in the school's assemblies, and run a kids' drama group.

I see my leadership role as first among many. We share leadership closely; you could have any one of us speaking and you'd get a similar picture. I'm a paid lay leader and everyone else is a volunteer. I'm the vision setter, lifting our eyes up and seeing where we're heading, not getting bogged down, and willing to be brave at times. During the pandemic, leading sensitively became more of a thing because people had other, weighty responsibilities at work, for example, and didn't need me adding to that. But we tried very hard not to lose the sense of something we're all very invested in. I try not to make big decisions without the team but sometimes I do need to go ahead and decide. The team is absolutely amazing and it's been thrilling to see them come alive and feel excited about faith.

I'm absolutely staggered because I always thought Gamston was very largely white, but we now have such an ethnically diverse congregation. I think that's partly because we have Victoria, whom I mentioned earlier, on the team and she's British-Chinese. She told us how she is acutely aware of walking in somewhere and wanting to see other people like her. So we started to explore diversity, prayed about it, and signed up as a Hong Kong Welcome Church.[1] This is bringing such joy and richness and wisdom into the church.

My vicar Mark is just brilliant. He has enabled Connect Gamston and is always available for a conversation, but he has also been very hands-off, and really trusts me to do things. I'm totally accountable to him and go to him a lot to ask questions and check we're on the right lines before we go ahead. He often has that nugget of wisdom I need. He's quite busy and it can be tricky to get dates in the diary, but I thank him a lot, particularly at the end of each year, because I couldn't do it without him.

We're trying to make prayer something we prioritise and have fun with together.

At Connect Gamston, we're trying to make prayer something we prioritise and have fun with together. Prayer is something that's evolving – we're not good at it – but I feel it's very important. Day-to-day prayer happens in all sorts of ways, like prayer-walking, praying as team, and at midweek groups. Every time I drive through Gamston, I pray. We've tried doing monthly prayer at different times of day, like prayer breakfasts on Saturday morning, and we did a 'prayer glow walk,'

1 www.welcomechurches.org/updates/hong-kong-ready-churches

wearing bright colours and holding lanterns, as a procession on Bonfire Night. On Fridays at midday, me and another lady take a pop-up banner to the canal path for 'Prayer on the Path.' We sit there with coffee and chat and offer prayer to people who pass. It's been really powerful and people know we're there praying for them. Despite being a middle-class area, where people can be quite guarded, they confide in us and it's such a privilege to pray for them and what and who they care about.

www.connectgamston.org

'Sarah is a visionary and creative leader with a great gift for connecting with people. She has set her heart on Jesus and inspires others to do the same.'
REVD MARK FRASER, Vicar, St Luke's Gamston

'Connect Gamston helped my family to settle in the new environment and develop a social network. More importantly, I have deepened my understanding of God and understood what I'm longing for.'
GERALD, Connect Gamston member

13

TERRY AND JILL HUGGINS

Upper Nar Garden Church, Norfolk

The Upper Nar Garden Church is bringing together people from scattered Norfolk villages. Despite Covid, this new worshipping community has built strong supportive relationships with each other, to explore faith, with any and all questions welcomed.

We retired back to Norfolk in 2016, where Terry is originally from and where we'd spent much of our married life. We're in the north-west of the county, between Norwich and King's Lynn, and we lead a small church in a network of Garden Churches. We first planted a church back in October 2019, asked to by the then vicar of the local benefice, a group of 17 churches, and the then diocese lead for church planting and revitalisation. This plant morphed into Upper Nar Garden Church just prior to Covid hitting.

The other Garden Churches in Norfolk are co-ordinated by Dave Lloyd, a good friend of ours in the Diocese of Norwich. We get together monthly with Dave and the other leaders, and we have a monthly gathering for all the people in the Garden Churches.

We operate in a very rural region, and yet within a stone's throw of where we're sitting, there are probably 20 churches. In an urban context with that many churches nearby, you'd expect there to be a variety and potential to find something that was attractive to you as a family or whatever. Here, all those churches provide more or less the same kind of thing. We're offering something different which may attract people who are not engaging with the other churches.

At Upper Nar, we meet once a month in person, when people travel from up to eight miles away, and we have a simple meal together. The other Wednesdays in the month, we meet on Zoom. The in-person format is similar to our Zoom meetings: we always have time to catch up with each other, we have worship with recorded songs, and we explore the Bible and pray together. One of our characteristics is to encourage contributions and questions a lot more than you would in a traditional service. We find that people appreciate space to ask questions and create discussion and for some, that's really important. People feel relaxed about asking anything and still being accepted at the end of it.

One of our characteristics is to encourage contributions and questions a lot more than you would in a traditional service.

The strength of Garden Church is relationship building. Because we meet so regularly, the friendships and relationships between the group have deepened. During the past 18 months, we've supported each other through bereavement, work issues, health and mental health challenges. Going through these difficult times has drawn us really close together. The support is genuine, not because it's expected. And we are vulnerable and honest with each other, there's no pretence – it's just us.

We get the most joy from these people – just walking with them through their lives as they grow and deepen their faith. That's been just wonderful to see. It's lovely because everybody is there because they want to be there, there's no sense of duty, that it's required of me to put on my Sunday best and go to church. And we have fun together! It's been harder on Zoom – when we do meet up, it's quite noticeable how the dynamic changes. In person, people open up more and are prepared to stay and chat much longer. Worship is different when we meet because we can sing together.

Demographically at Upper Nar, we're typically at the older end of the spectrum, around the ages of 40–70. We're about 14 in number now; probably half of those go to another church on Sunday and for the rest, the Garden Church is their church. We do our absolute best to avoid putting people into any sort of conflict in having to choose between the two. There have been various discussions in our diocese about what Garden Church is. How does it work? We're very insistent that Garden Church meets during the week and there is no requirement for you to go to a 'proper church' on a Sunday.

Garden Church meets during the week and there is no requirement for you to go to a 'proper church' on a Sunday.

The biggest challenge is finding a way to get in touch with the local communities. There are quite a number of retired people like us in the area but also a reasonable demographic of young- to midlife-marrieds, with children of school age. That's the group we would really like to reach and that's the biggest challenge we've found, across such a dispersed area. Terry walks around with the dog and sees families out but there's nowhere to get to know them, and there's no church that appears to be attracting them. We've taken part in village events and activities but we have to focus on just one village at a time because that's as much resource as we can muster.

Some people can be traditional in their views and they tend to associate church with the building, so they don't quite understand what we're about. Most of the local churches are struggling for numbers but we don't see ourselves as a threat, although maybe we are seen a little bit that way. Most of the people we would encourage to join us would probably never join a traditional church. We're certainly not trying to steal people away from these congregations and we want to keep good relationship with these churches.

When you're planting in a rural area, you have to be patient and focus not on numbers but on the quality of what you build. The biggest thing is you have to like people. We've built a little community, they're all very special to us, and we love them for the people they are. They're all focused on Jesus and want to know more about him. Some would say they are further away and struggle with doubts, others are more certain, but they are all walking towards Jesus in the centre. That's the important thing – there's no other requirement of them.

www.garden-church.org/upper-nar

'Seeing God at work in the small, simple, organic, "unchoreographed" life of the missional community has been so inspiring. To just practise the basic ingredients of invitational Christian community together and in turn see unexpected and exciting fruit restores the wonder of the gospel. Something of the essence of church has been restored. In some ways it feels like we are all learning what it means to be church again. Removing the buildings and budgets to prioritise the basics has shown us new treasures.'

REVD DAVID LLOYD, Lead Practitioner for Church Planting, Diocese of Norwich

'Upper Nar is somewhere I can look at what faith is really about, away from the man-made rituals of church, simply searching with others to find the Jesus way of living life.'

HELEN, Upper Nar Garden Church member

14

FRAN CARABOTT

St Margaret's, Portsmouth

'We're an unlikely group of people with an unlikely leader!' says lay pioneer minister Fran Carabott, who leads a Portsmouth church plant that has become a community hub. St Margaret's approach is 'come as you are – no perfect people allowed.' Fran recounts this church's story of transformation.

I'd say this is the most exciting thing I've ever done. Five years ago, St Margaret's was closed and deemed unsafe. Sometimes I get quite emotional when I walk into the church, thinking back to when there was water pouring into this completely shut building and how there was no life – and now people are meeting God in this place. It's incredibly powerful, this transformation, which has started to spill out into the community. Now if you mention St Margaret's, everyone around here knows that it's a church that is active and alive. They're seeing a space that was desolate come back to life.

At the first meeting, everyone was looking at me and saying, 'What's the plan?' – and there was no plan!

In early 2017, Mike Duff, the vicar from our sending church St Jude's, approached me and my wife Clare and asked if we'd be interested in planting a church. I had been a Christian for about 20 years but I guess he saw me as a bit of a rough diamond. He said no one else wants to put their hand up for this, but I said, 'I do!' Clare and I agreed straight away, we didn't even really think about it. We made an announcement at church that we were going to meet in St Margaret's community hall every week and pray. At the first meeting, everyone was looking at me and saying, 'What's the plan?' – and there was no plan! But as the weeks went on, God gave us a vision and real heart for this community. Me, Mike, and a team member who's now our operations manager went on The Plant Course from the Gregory Centre for Church Multiplication,[1] which helped us develop this vision as well as testing its viability.

In October 2017, we launched a 4 p.m. service, meeting in the tiny community hall. I think 75 people came that day, but we came back to reality the next Sunday when there were only 25 of us. But you keep going, don't you, and it has slowly grown over the years. The vision developed and we started doing outreach, Alpha, a toddler group, constantly looking outwards. We were all volunteers – I continued to run my property maintenance company while leading the church. I think my entrepreneurial spirit has actually been a help.

In November 2017, I was in the discernment process for ordination and had a local pre-BAP. I thought it went really well but they said I wasn't Anglican enough! So I said to myself, 'Here I am, we've just launched the church, and God, I know you've called me here, so I'll just carry on.' About eight months later, Joanne Grenfell, our archdeacon visited. She said what we were doing was amazing. She found funding for us and got me licensed in 2018 as a lay pioneer minister. The diocese paid me for two and a half days a week, so I still had to work in my own business to supplement our income. Two years ago, I got a training grant through St Mellitus College[2] so I was finally able to stop work in order to study and run the church. In 2020, I was recommended for ordination training, and I'm now in my final year.

St Margaret's is in a mixed community on a road with shops and two-up, two-down terraced houses, as well as big houses on

1 The Plant Course is a practical, encouraging, and stretching course to equip church planters and their teams. It's designed for churches who are ready to plant in the next six to 12 months and have their bishop's or denominational authority's approval. www.ccx.org.uk/plant
2 www.stmellitus.ac.uk

the seafront. It's quite diverse, ethnically and socially. We seem to mainly attract people with no church background or those who have fallen away from faith and church. Our age range is wide, from newborn to 92. We got some money from SDF[3] which meant we could renovate the building, but we had to move in before the work was finished because we got too big for the community hall. So we were in the church for one and a half years, freezing cold, with one loo! Now we've got heating and the church is used seven days a week.

We seem to mainly attract people with no church background or those who have fallen away from faith and church.

Everyone says how welcome they feel when they first come to St Margaret's. Our approach is 'come as you are – no perfect people allowed' and we get feedback that we're all 'normal'! We've created the culture right from the start that everyone is on the welcome team, so if someone is new, go and chat to them. We've got a café, a shop, a food bank, and a soft play centre in the church. We encourage our members to go and share their story of finding Jesus and quite often you hear our teams during the week saying, 'We'd love to see you on a Sunday' and talking about what goes on at church. That's been really wonderful. There are lots of opportunities for people to volunteer, and you don't have to be a Christian to be involved, but we've found that some of our volunteers are becoming Christians. Last year we baptised eight adults during lockdown and 33 new people joined the church. Amazing.

When we first started, it was challenging because all our finances had to go through St Jude's and it really slowed things up, but now we have own PCC [Parochial Church Council]. St Jude's associate vicar is my training incumbent and he just lets me get on with it. He supports me when I need it and is a real cheerleader and enabler. Diocesan support has increased over the years and they support us tremendously, which is really encouraging. We're planting again in October 2022 on Eastney

3 Strategic Development Funding. www.churchofengland.org/about/renewal-reform/funding-mission-and-growth/strategic-development-funding

estate, less than a mile from St Margaret's. It has always been our desire to plant again, and God broke my heart for that particular area. We have one family who live on the estate and we hope to start with 10–15 people in a community centre there.

We launched a morning service last year, so now we have about 95 people between the two services. The morning service is just half an hour because our heart is to reach new people, who may not want to sit in church for too long, and we didn't want to attract a load of people from other churches. That's worked well – most people who have joined are completely new to faith. We meet at 9.30 a.m. for breakfast and then at 10 a.m. we gather to worship together for half an hour, which includes time for prayer and discussion. Then we open the soft play area and café and conversations can continue. Our other service is at 4 p.m., and that's an hour long. That one attracts a real mix of people.

The morning service is just half an hour because our heart is to reach new people, who may not want to sit in church for too long.

Right from the start, I realised that I needed to empower people to preach and lead, which has worked really well, and all our services have been lay led. We've got 10 midweek life groups, and I meet regularly with the leaders to encourage and support them. One of our leaders, Sam, is a very gifted evangelist and he has been journeying with us, as my apprentice. He's now on the ordination discernment process. We've been blessed with an operations manager, who's SDF-funded, and we have Sue, who looks after admin and finances.

Sue lives in the cottages next to the church and when we launched, I knocked on the door and introduced myself. I remember her coming up to me after eight months and thanking me for what a difference the church had made to the community. I invited her to an Alpha course but an hour before, she texted me to say she wasn't going to come and I was very disappointed. But I never gave up on her and eventually she came to a service. I sat next to her at the end of the service and she burst into tears, ended up doing the Alpha course, and got baptised last year. Her life has been completely transformed by Jesus. Sue's story is one of many like this, of people meeting Jesus, and we praise God for each and every one.

www.stmagscc.uk

'When I first met Fran, it was clear he believed he was called to plant a church and that he had a huge gift for coming alongside people and loving them, with all their doubts and imperfections. My task as archdeacon was to clear as many obstacles from his path as possible – for Fran as a lay church planter and in the discernment process, and also around the reopening and restoration of St Margaret's building. He and the team have done something amazing, and have a built a welcoming, loving, growing community of faithful people. St Margaret's has had new life breathed into it.'

RT REVD DR JOANNE GRENFELL, former Archdeacon of Portsdown and now Bishop of Stepney

'Being a part of the St Mag's family and saying yes to accepting Jesus in my life has given me a real sense of peace, focus, and direction that I've never known before.'

SUE, St Margaret's member

15

LIZZIE LOWRIE

StoryHouse, Crosby

Lizzie and Dave Lowrie's town-centre coffee shop serves ethical coffee and cinnamon buns and welcomes young adults with friendship and everyday faith, over a latte.

We started StoryHouse coffee shop in Crosby because we felt the church we were then part of wasn't connecting effectively with younger generations. Mission and evangelism has changed – it's much more relational now, not just about inviting people to events. Fewer young people are growing up in church and even expecting them to walk through a church door is a massive ask. Church is a different culture: When do you stand up? When do you sit down? What do the words mean? We wanted to create a space to build relationships with our community and then introduce people to Jesus from that relationship, rather than an invitation.

Mission and evangelism has changed – it's much more relational now.

I'm a lay leader and my husband Dave is an ordained pioneer minister. We moved to Crosby in 2014 for Dave's curacy, with the remit to start something for people who weren't coming to church. I was originally funded by SDF money from the Joshua Centre, part of the Diocese of Liverpool, but that ended so now we're self-supporting.

In 2016, we heard very clearly from God that we should start a coffee shop, as well as a church. Someone who didn't know us at all prayed over us and said, 'You're thinking about opening a coffee shop and you need to do it!' This was a bit controversial because the church we were at in Crosby had a café that had been going for years, but it wasn't ever going to attract young people. We'd opened a café in Chester back in 2007 as a mission base, but after 10 months we ran out of money. However, we knew the concept worked because people had come to faith.

As pioneers, we had something that we thought of as normal but is not: being able to imagine what's not there yet. So we opened our coffee shop in Crosby town centre, known as Crosby Village, and after nearly a year of building relationships with customers, we began to meet as a small congregation in the shop.

As pioneers, we had something that we thought of as normal but is not: being able to imagine what's not there yet.

When we launched, the town was mainly empty shop units and the community really lamented the demise of the area and how it used to be buzzing. As followers of Jesus, we wanted to do that Jeremiah 29 thing – seek the prosperity of the city, be part of the revival of the community, and draw people back into it. With a coffee shop, it is so important to have footfall, and we're right in the centre, in a significant location. In the five years since we opened, Crosby Village has undergone a significant regeneration, with shop units restored and filled with local businesses. Crosby Village is now a buzzing centre, which we consider a big answer to prayer.

Unlike church, everyone knows what to do in a coffee shop – you go in, you buy a drink, you sit down. We call it StoryHouse because it's a place where people can share their story and find their place in God's story. With traditional church models, even church plants, the Christians can often feel like the hosts, but we wanted to receive more from people coming through the door, to hear what their lives are like and not assume what they want or need to hear from us. We also wanted the space to illustrate the creativity of God in a contemporary way. After all, stained glass windows were originally designed to creatively tell the story of God.

Going into a space that's informal, that's creative and relaxed is everything that a lot of people don't see church as being –

we wanted this to be our base for mission. We've worked with creative people to create a really cool space that people want to hang out in. When we do Alpha, it's somewhere you want to be and invite your friends to, not a dusty church hall.

Since lockdown, we've kept the number of seats in the café to 35, and we're open Monday to Saturday. When you come in, there's a chalkboard with details of what's happening in the StoryHouse community, including a storytime for children, and what's happening at StoryHouse Church. We get our coffee from an ethical supplier and claim to serve the best church coffee ever! Among other things, we serve cinnamon buns we bake here, and a croissant loaf, which is terribly unhealthy but absolutely delicious – like a bread and butter pudding made with croissants and chocolate!

When we first started, we didn't have much Christian stuff around because we wanted to build relationships first and for people to know that we weren't weird, simple as that. There was a very soft spiritual touch, like framed quotes from people like C. S. Lewis on the wall. In designing the space, we thought about the flow and being relational, so – and this sounds a small thing – the coffee machine isn't between the barista and the customer, it's to the side so they can have a conversation.

We call our staff 'evangelist baristas' and we have seven on team, full-time and part-time, who are in their 20s. Quite a few staff come from big city-centre churches in Liverpool, and we think it's a really great practical mission training model. They're not just making coffee but they're being discipled and growing spiritually. Dave and I are co-leaders of StoryHouse Church; he is senior manager of the coffee shop and I am the creative prayer and mission lead, and train the staff. This includes what we call 'missional listening,' thinking about who is coming through the door and how can we connect with them. What gifts and passions can our baristas use for mission in a relational way?

We had to shut during lockdown so we put a lot of content online. We started to create resources that are well-designed and use informal language to help people engage with faith in a new way. We ran the 24-7 Prayer Course[1] and I created a series of postcards on how to pray. Because there is a large Catholic community in Liverpool, people are often familiar with prayer here. Because, by this point, we'd established ourselves in the community and people knew us, we streamed Sunday church on our café social media platforms. The church actually grew during lockdown as quite a few 20-somethings who loved the café started watching church online and joined us. They had an on-and-off faith background and said they'd been thinking about coming to StoryHouse Church but it meant getting up on a Sunday, so just being able to watch the service from the comfort of their home really helped. We've got about 55 adults and 20+ children at church now.

The church actually grew during lockdown as quite a few 20-somethings who loved the café started watching church online.

Once a year, we run Alpha in the evenings in the café, and I've also created a pre-Alpha course, because Alpha does assume quite a bit of faith knowledge. We've run it once so far – it's called 'Story of your Life' – and it takes the principles of what makes a good story and applies those to our individual stories. We used examples of stories from the Bible as well as from movies, and framed it with themes like redemption, purpose, and community. It really attracted young adults and we will do it again, once we've tweaked it to add a bit more faith content. We've got an upstairs space above the café, which we'd like to develop as a prayer room, run arts and crafts clubs, provide space for kids revising for exams, and maybe a co-working area for those working from home.

In the 14 years we've been pioneers, we've learned that you really need the support of ordained people. For instance, celebrating communion can be a challenge for church plants, unless they happen to have someone ordained on the team, as we do with Dave. It's also important to learn from people, lay and ordained, who have started stuff themselves. You need champions and people who not only understand the institution

1 www.prayercourse.org

but who 'get it' and will give you freedom to experiment and not be prescriptive. Some of our most significant support actually came from outside the Anglican Church, from a Newfrontiers[2] church that was thinking about planting in Crosby. They were absolutely amazing, giving two families their blessing to move to StoryHouse, which meant us gaining and them losing significant giving, and sending musicians to support our worship. It was a really great example of growing the kingdom of God together, and not about denominations.

As well as the incredible people God has brought into our lives through StoryHouse, what's really energising is having the freedom to think creatively about what's possible and try stuff out. We just go for it – it's given us a lot of flexibility. Not knowing what's next can be stressful but it's also really fun. It's a case of partnering with God, what he's doing here, and leaning into that.

www.storyhouse.community

> *'The most inspiring thing for me is how StoryHouse has been so effective at connecting with so many local people. It was their vision, not mine – my only role was to cheer them on and help them succeed.'*
>
> DAN ROGERS, Director, Joshua Centre, Diocese of Liverpool
>
> *'StoryHouse's living message of Jesus' love and grace has transformed my life through freedom. Freed of sin, fear, doubt, shame, and guilt, I now know contentment.'*
>
> NIGEL, StoryHouse member

2 www.newfrontierstogether.org

16

IDINA DUNMORE

The Table, Southall, West London

Meeting to make friends, eat a meal together, and explore faith is the DNA of The Table, which has become a new worshipping community for people of different faith backgrounds. Idina finds that serving local people and churches has been key in creating Christian community.

I moved to Southall in 2008 with four others, explicitly to start a missional community. We were bi-vocational – we worked to support ourselves and gave the rest of our time to the community and whatever God brought to our doorstep, on the estate where we were living. At the time, I was working with teenage parents as a health visitor and I spent eight years as part of this community, getting to know our neighbours, and loving and serving them.

Before we moved to Southall, I spoke with the vicar of St John's, Southall Green, about us moving into the area as a missional community. She said, *It was a wise thing to do, going beforehand with an idea, rather than turning up and saying, 'We're here!'* 'Why don't you speak at the front one Sunday and ask people what they think?' I did and the response was really positive, with people saying this is what we really need. That felt like such a welcome and I think it was a wise thing to do, going beforehand with an idea, rather than turning up and saying, 'We're here!'

For the first year, our model was just to serve the local churches and do whatever would help them. We focused on outward-looking ministries at St John's, and with others, started

Messy Church and a toddler group. We also offered some of our time to start a homeless night shelter in partnership with other churches.

The idea for The Table came about in 2017, when people who had been coming to our house for a weekly community meal, as well as those attending our various community ministries, were asking about Jesus and joining in prayer with us.

The most important thing to say about The Table is it's centred round a meal. You can't meet in Southall without food! People bring food from lots of different cultures – we have rice and dahl, Indian curries, noodle dishes. Your plate is piled with all sorts of delicious things. We ask people to bring food or drink, and that could just be a packet of biscuits, but it means everyone can contribute. After food, we look at a few Bible verses together and discuss them. Those days, when we're sitting around a table discussing things, I absolutely love. There might be a woman from a Muslim background, a Persian asylum seeker, and someone from the Punjab and they're all discussing the story of Jesus and praying together. That's the joy for me, seeing people grow in their interest and faith in Jesus.

The most important thing to say about The Table is it's centred round a meal.

Southall has a diverse religious and cultural mix. Sikhs are in the majority, followed by Muslims – together they make up to 70 per cent of the population. At least half of St John's congregation are from an Asian background. While some people who come to The Table also visit St John's, for most, Sunday morning church isn't an entirely comfortable space for them. So we launched as a small Friday evening group, meeting in the parish hall, and the other weeks of the month, we meet in a home. We get up to 15 in someone's home and 30–40 when we meet in the hall. Numbers have dropped since lockdown and it's also very weather-dependent.

We had a Sikh gentleman who was part of The Table, very much a spiritual seeker. He still went to the gurdwara but would talk about how much he loved Jesus and would pray with us. He'd come to nearly all our events and bring his friends. He loved us and we loved him. Sadly, he passed away and I was invited to give the eulogy at his Sikh funeral. I was able to talk about Christian hope. Being there, alongside his friends, was a really special privilege. Baptising four people was another memorable moment – an Iranian mother and her two teenage children, and a young man. They gave beautiful testimonies about finding Jesus.

It's also been a really wonderful thing to encourage leaders from different backgrounds, particularly UKME. There are seven of us in The Table's co-ordinating team and we're also heavily involved at St John's, because we're a new St John's congregation, rather than a separate church. We create vision together, share out leading at our gatherings, and encourage people who come along to lead too. We try to make things very informal. There are always struggles in a leadership team, aren't there, but we keep working at it and try to understand and encourage each other. I quite like a flat hierarchy and I'm probably not a decisive leader; I'd rather get there by consensus, which takes a longer time. We have different ethoses among the team about whether The Table is there to prepare people to go to church, or if The Table as a congregation is enough in itself. That's an ongoing discussion.

There are always struggles in a leadership team, aren't there, but we keep working at it and try to understand and encourage each other.

In 2016 I began the discernment process for ordination as a pioneer minister. I trained as an ordinand with Church Mission Society (CMS)[1] and really enjoyed it, meeting similar-minded people from lay and ordained backgrounds. It's very mission-focused – my course was an MA in pioneer leadership, alongside ministerial training. I became a curate in 2019 and asked London Diocese to allow me to join CMS' pioneer training, alongside my traditional curacy.

1 www.churchmissionsociety.org

I'm going to be moving to a new role in the summer of 2022. It's still to be worked out but I'll probably be working out of a different church, as a pioneer minister across the wider Southall area. So I'll be handing over leadership of The Table to a couple of people on the co-ordinating team and looking to expand the team. Coming out of lockdown, we need to consolidate The Table and new leaders will hopefully take it on to a new stage.

People have asked me if I'll take The Table model into my new role and plant one somewhere else. I think I have more of a heart to ask people, in their own context, what God is doing there and where do they want to start. I think we have a good model with The Table but the next thing might look completely different. It's about seeing where God is at work and joining in.

www.stjohnsouthall.org.uk/our-ministries

'It's been wonderful to see The Table develop into a safe, nurturing, and prayerful space for people from diverse cultural backgrounds to connect together and learn from one another about Jesus. Its charisms are a celebration of the good news for the poor, welcoming the stranger, and generous hospitality for those on the margins of society. The Table is a beautiful Spirit-filled space where people can be honest about their vulnerabilities and find that God's light shines through the broken cracks of our lives.

I have seen my role in terms of permission-giving, being a supportive back-up who encourages creativity and risk-taking, being an advocate for Idina's ministry and The Table in the wider church community, and emphasising that the most important thing is to be authentic to who God has called us to be, rather than being anxious about meeting targets or delivering measurable results.'

REVD ANNA POULSON, Vicar, St John's Southall Green

'At The Table I experience God in the boisterous laughter and play of the children. I experience God in the people sitting around and talking to each other. I experience God in the hymns that we sing: my favourite is "Bless the Lord, oh my soul." I also experience God looking at the food that people have brought to share, that's part of God's blessing. I've always left The Table energised and feeling positive.

Through the discussions, I understand Jesus more. He went through so much: being homeless, being rejected, being a refugee, being ostracised and tortured. And even being mocked. And betrayed by his followers. So, I think this is the beauty of The Table, we are exploring Jesus on a very beautiful level, in the sense that I would say I have come closer to him, and I can understand why his message resonates with millions of people around the world.'

The Table member

the Gregory
**centre for
church
multiplication**

Myriad serves the mixed ecology vision
and strategy of the Church of England by shining
a light on the new forms of churches that are being planted,
learning lessons, thinking through complex challenges
and providing resources for the support and training
of lay people to form new church communities.
It is a central part of the work of The Gregory Centre
for Church Multiplication (CCX) which is led by Rt Revd
Ric Thorpe, the Bishop of Islington. CCX supports leaders,
church teams and dioceses across London, England and
beyond as they multiply disciples, churches and networks.
It equips and resources the Church to reach new people
in new and renewed ways. Whilst it is a part of the Church
of England, the Gregory Centre for Church Multiplication
works with many denominations and networks.

For more information,
scan the QR code or visit:

ccx.org.uk

CCX.media

CCX.media is a resource hub to inspire, provoke and equip you to multiply.

Every resource we create is now accessible in one place; with hundreds of products and contributors, there is something here for you wherever you are on your planting journey.

Choose the membership option that works for you and get equipped to play your part.

For more information,
scan the QR code or visit:

ccx.media

VIDEOS

RESOURCES

LIVESTREAMS

COURSES

CONFERENCES

BOOKS

Written by Ric Thorpe, the Church of England's bishop for church planting, this book looks at the biblical, theological and historical roots of resource churches.

It covers all the practicalities of how to launch and grow an effective resource church, and draws on Ric's extensive experience, practical wisdom and advice for church teams and diocesan leaders.

It is full of stories from those who have planted and lead resource churches, together with reflections from each of their bishops. Although the book is written from an Anglican perspective, its principles may be applied to similar churches in other denominations and sections of the church.

For more information,
scan the QR code or visit:

ccx.media

Printed in Great Britain
by Amazon